THE SMOKED
DELIGHT

How to Prepare Delicious Wood
Pellet Grill Meals and Become a Smoking
Master in No Time.
With Vegetarian Dishes!

Phil Robson

CONTENTS

What is a Wood Pellet Grill?

Are you asking what a wood pellet grill is? At least we assume you asked, so we can finish this part earlier: A wood pellet grill is a combination of an electric grill and a wood fired grill that smokes food at a constant temperature by means of a fire driven by wood pellets, the temperature being regulated by the amount of pellets burned.

If you have access to a power socket and a few pounds of good quality wood pellets, you can use a pellet grill to make the best ribs, steaks, roasts, or any other grilled or smoked dishes, even if you are not much of a grill master. Simply put, wood pellet grills take the hassle out of smoking meat, traditionally the most challenging part of grilling.

How Does It Work?

Before we move on to the advantages of a pellet grill compared to a charcoal or gas grill, let's talk about what actually happens in a pellet grill. When you turn on the grill and set the desired temperature, an auger (basically a long screw) starts turning in the base of the grill. The wood pellets that you have placed in the mound are slowly fed into the firebox, where they are ignited by the electric heating element. At higher temperatures, the auger feeds more pellets into the chamber; when less heat is needed (as you prefer), it feeds fewer pellets.

The heat of the fire is promoted by a fan, and the same internal fan that adds air to the flames also helps to circulate the heat and smoke produced by the pellets around your meat (or other foods, but mainly meat), ensuring saturation of aroma and flavor. As the heat is generated in the combustion chamber and spread by convection, the temperature is mostly constant throughout the grill, so you don't have to keep opening the lid and checking things.

To be honest, if you have a stockpile filled with sufficient wood pellets, a good knowledge of the target temperatures and the approximate time needed to reach them, you can cook most of the time with a good pellet grill, without the help of your hands.

Advantages of a Wood Pellet Grill Over a Traditional Grill

A pellet grill really has countless advantages over traditional grills or smokers. You will realize this immediately upon first use, nevertheless we list the main ones:

- Precise temperature control to allow long, slow cooking and smoking or quick searing.
- Wide temperature range, typically 180°F to 500°F
- Control of the flavor profile according to the pellets selected.
- Indirect heat preventing ignition and uneven cooking.
- Easy start-up and easy cleaning.

Which Wood Pellet Grill Should I Choose?

There are many excellent pellet grills available and if you don't buy a budget unit, you will get a decent grill for sure. Rather than saying you should just go with Traeger, which is probably the first name in pellet grills, or Pit Boss, which makes amazing combos, or Country Smokers, which has some great little smokers, let's talk about the different types of pellet grills you can get, without any favoritism.

If you are looking for the best wood pellet grill that most people imagine when they close their eyes and think of a pellet grill, the **Traeger Pro 575** is the perfect choice. Its large 18 lbs. pellet hopper allows you to smoke for hours, and its large grill surface can hold up to five ribs.

For a smaller smoker who can easily stow it in the trunk and take it to the park, campsite, or to a party for fun (of course you'll need a plug socket or generator), the **Country Smokers Frontier Series The Traveler** is an affordable and great choice. It can cook almost a dozen burgers or a whole rack of ribs, and the 3.5 lbs. tank can keep you warm for at least two hours without refilling on moderate heat settings.

If you like the idea of a combination smoker and gas grill, allowing you to smoke slowly on one side and sear steaks quickly on the other, the **Pit Boss Sportsman Pellet/Gas Combo** is surprisingly good value for money, but bear in mind that you have a much smaller smoking surface than with a pellet grill of the same physical size.

Finally, the **Green Mountain Grills Davy Crockett** pellet grill can run on a 12-volt battery and has a large temperature range of 150°F to 550°F, allowing you to grill on a boat, at the campsite unplugged, or during a power outage.

Which Pellets Should I Choose?

All pellet grills use the same size wood pellets, and all reputable brands offer food-safe wood that provides comparable burn times and heat, so you don't have to think too much about which brand to choose for your grill's wood pellets.

However, you need to think long and hard about what flavors and aroma profile you want for the meat you are smoking.

For ribs, chops and pork in general, a savory smoke is best - think hickory or mesquite, the latter having a stronger flavor profile and the former better for long, slow smoking.

For grilling beef, pecan, maple or other woods that are sweeter are ideal for balancing the bold flavor that characterizes this type of meat.

For chicken or other poultry, you can play around as you would with frying, roasting or other preparations of this kind of meat, which is essentially a blank canvas. Cherry pellets can add sweetness, alder wood can add smoke, and pecans or other nuts can add a spicy nutty flavor that will sink deep into the meat.

CHAPTER 1. STARTERS

1.1 Mandarin Wings

Preparation time: 5 minutes

Cooking time: 30 minutes

Servings: 2

Ingredients

- One bottle mandarin orange sauce
- Two tbsp chicken rub
- Two lbs. chicken wings, drumettes separated

Steps

- In a bowl, coat the chicken wings in the mandarin sauce. Sprinkle the chicken rub onto the wings, mix well & marinate for 30 minutes.
- Set the grill temperature to 350°F, then keep the lid closed for 15 minutes.
- Put the marinated wings straight on the hot grill grates & cook for thirty minutes. Serve.

1.2 Grilled Teff Flatbread with Cilantro Sauce

Preparation time: 5 minutes

Cooking time: 30 minutes

Servings: 2

Ingredients

Flatbread

- Half cup teff flour
- One and three quarters cups water
- Half tsp salt
- One egg
- Olive oil

Cilantro Sauce

- Four garlic cloves, chopped
- Two bunches fresh coriander, chopped
- Two Jalapeño peppers, seeded & chopped
- One tsp kosher salt
- One tsp ground cardamom
- One tsp ground cumin
- Half tsp red pepper Flakes
- Three quarters cup olive oil
- Three quarters cup lemon juice

Steps

- Combine the 1-3/4 cups water & teff flour in a glass bowl. Cover Loosely & let it rise overnight in a warm place.
- Set the grill temperature to 350°F, place a cast-iron pan on the grill, then keep the lid closed for 15 minutes to preheat.
- Whisk the egg into the fermented tuff & season with the salt. Lightly oil the cast iron pan. Once the oil is hot, add a small amount of batter to the skillet, instantly turning the pan around to coat.
- Cook till the bread has firmed. Repeat with the rest of the batter. Prepare the sauce: blend all the ingredients in a food processor till smooth. Serve with the hot bread.

1.3 Bacon Wrapped Chicken Wings

Preparation time: 30 minutes

Cooking time: 1 hour

Servings: 6

Ingredients

- Two lbs. chicken wings
- Three cups beer
- Two tsp red pepper flakes
- One lb. bacon strips
- Two tbsp chicken rub

Steps

- Cut the tips from the wings & throw them away.
- Put the wings & red pepper flakes in a large bowl & cover with the beer. Refrigerate overnight.
- Remove the wings from the brine & pat dry. Top generously with chicken rub.
- Wrap each wing with a bacon strip.
- Set the grill temperature to 450°F, then keep the lid closed for 15 minutes.
- Put the wings straight on the hot grill grate, close the lid & cook for around thirty minutes. Turn the wings & cook for thirty minutes more or till the bacon becomes crispy & the chicken is completely cooked. Serve.

1.4 Grilled Shrimp Cocktail

Preparation time: 5 minutes

Cooking time: 10 minutes

Servings: 2

Ingredients

Main

- Two lbs. shrimp
- Two tbsp olive oil
- One tsp Old Bay seasoning
- Italian Parsley, minced

Cocktail Sauce

- Half cup ketchup
- Two tbsp prepared horseradish
- Two tbsp lemon juice
- Ground black pepper
- Kosher salt

Steps

- Set the grill temperature to 350°F, then keep the lid closed for 15 minutes.
- Shell & devein the shrimps, leaving the tails on. Mix the shrimp with oil & Old Bay seasoning in a large bowl. Put the shrimp on a cookie sheet.
- Put the cookie sheet on the grill grate & cook till opaque, around five to seven minutes.
- Prepare the cocktail sauce: combine horseradish, lemon juice & ketchup. Season with pepper & salt.
- In a bowl, pour the cocktail sauce on the grilled shrimp. Season the shrimps with minced parsley. Serve.

1.5 Grilled Shrimp Brochette

Preparation time: 20 minutes

Cooking time: 20 minutes

Servings: 6

Ingredients

- One lb. large shrimps, shelled & deveined
- Six jalapeño peppers
- Eight oz Monterey Jack Cheese
- One lb. bacon
- Two tbsp all-purpose rub

- Fillet the shrimps, slightly flatten & set aside. Core & seed the jalapeños & slice them into tiny slivers. Cut the cheese in pieces the same size as the peppers. Cut in half the bacon slices.
- Put one jalapeño slice & one cheese slice inside each shrimp. Wrap every stuffed shrimp in the half bacon piece.
- Season the shrimps with the all-purpose rub.
- Set the grill temperature to 400°F, then keep the lid closed for 15 minutes.
- Put the shrimps straight on the slightly oiled grill grate. Cook for around twenty minutes, flipping once, till the shrimps change color & the bacon gets crisp.
- Take the shrimps from the grill & let rest for 10 minutes. Serve.

1.6 Roasted Garlic Herb Potatoes

Preparation time: 30 minutes

Cooking time: 45 minutes

Servings: 4

Ingredients

- Four large potatoes
- One tsp salt
- Two tbsp olive oil
- One tsp rosemary, minced
- One tsp thyme, minced
- Two garlic cloves, minced
- Two tsp flake salt
- One tsp chopped parsley

Steps

- Set the grill temperature to 400°F, then keep the lid closed for 15 minutes.
- Cut potatoes into wedges & place them into cold water with 1 tsp salt for half an hour.

- Mix the rosemary, oil, garlic & thyme in a big bowl. Take the potatoes from the frost water & dry them completely.
- Toss the potatoes in the oil mixture & put them on a parchment-lined cookie sheet, in a single layer. Season with flake salt.
- Put the cookie sheets on the grill grate & roast for thirty minutes; turn the potatoes & cook for fifteen more minutes until golden & crispy.
- Take the potatoes from the grill, sprinkle with parsley & serve with your favorite dipping sauce.

1.7 Grilled Prosciutto Asparagus

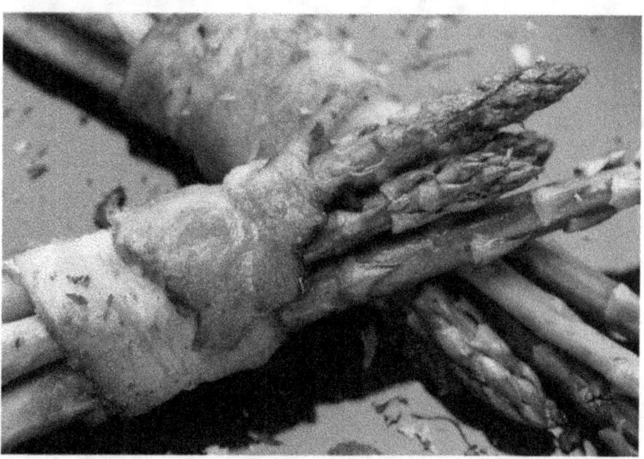

Preparation time: 20 minutes

Cooking time: 15 minutes

Servings: 6

Ingredients

- Two bunches asparagus
- Salt & Pepper
- Four oz prosciutto
- Olive oil
- Zest of one lemon
- Two tbsp balsamic vinegar, divided
- Three tbsp toasted pine nuts

- Set the grill temperature to 400°F, then keep the lid closed for 15 minutes.
- Wash the asparagus & pat dry. Cut the bottom thirds of the stalks & throw them away.
- Wrap a prosciutto slice around four to five stalks & put them on a parchment-lined cookie sheet. Sprinkle the asparagus with salt, olive oil, lemon zest & pepper.
- Put the cookie sheet on the grill grate & close the lid. After five minutes, flip the asparagus & drizzle with one tbsp of the balsamic vinegar.
- Close the lid again & cook till the prosciutto becomes crispy & the asparagus is completely cooked, around five to eight minutes.
- Sprinkle the asparagus with pine nuts & drizzle with the leftover balsamic vinegar. Serve.

1.8 Smoked Guacamole

Preparation time: 20 minutes

Cooking time: 15 minutes

Servings: 6

Ingredients

- Seven cored & peeled avocados, halved
- One whole chile poblano
- Four ears corn, husked
- One quarter cup cilantro, chopped
- One quarter cup tomato, chopped
- One quarter cup red onion, chopped
- Two tbsp lime juice
- One tsp ground cumin
- One tbsp garlic, minced
- Chile powder to taste
- Pepper & salt, to taste

- Set the grill temperature to 180°F, then keep the lid closed for 15 minutes.
- Put the avocados halves cut side up & smoke for ten minutes.
- Take the avocados from the grill & increase the temperature to 450°F.
- Put the corn & poblano pepper straight on the grill grate. Cook for fifteen to twenty minutes until charred.
- Take the corn from the cobs & set aside.
- Put the hot poblano pepper in a small bowl, cover with cling film & wait for ten minutes; the skin should peel off easily. Chop the pepper & add it to the corn kernels.
- Mash the smoked avocados in a large mixing bowl, leaving some chunks. Add the corn, peppers & all leftover ingredients. Mix & season with salt & pepper. Serve.

1.9 Grilled Sweet Potatoes

Preparation time: 5 minutes

Cooking time: 20 minutes

Servings: 6

Ingredients

- Five large, sweet potatoes
- One tbsp olive oil
- One tsp salt

- One tsp ground black pepper
- Half tsp onion powder

- Clean the sweet potatoes, peel them, & cut into eighths lengthwise.
- Put the slices in a bowl & season with salt, oil, onion powder & pepper, mixing thoroughly.
- Set the grill temperature to 480°F, then keep the lid closed for 15 minutes.
- Put the sweet potatoes wedges directly on the hot grill grate, cook for 35-40 minutes & serve.

1.10 Smoked Artichoke Dip

Preparation time: 15 minutes

Cooking time: 1 hour

Servings: 8

Ingredients

- Ten garlic cloves
- Half cup parmesan cheese
- Olive oil
- Half cup cheddar cheese
- Half cup fontina cheese
- Half cup provolone cheese
- Half cup cream cheese
- Half cup mayonnaise
- One can artichokes
- Kosher salt
- Ground black pepper

Steps

- Set the grill temperature to 350°F, then keep the lid closed for 15 minutes.
- In a small oven-safe pan, put garlic cloves & add sufficient olive oil to cover the garlic. Move it on grill & cook for around 35 to 40 minutes. Garlic will be done when soft enough to smash with a fork. Take it from the grill & allow it to cool.
- Drain the garlic & reserve the oil for another recipe. Put the garlic in a bowl & smash with the fork till it becomes a paste.
- Combine the cheddar, parmesan, fontina & provolone cheeses. Reserve half cup of the mixture.
- Mix the cheese mixture with the mayonnaise, cream cheese, artichokes & garlic. Season with salt & pepper & mix thoroughly.
- Put the mixture in an oven-safe dish & sprinkle with the reserved half cup of cheese mixture. Put the dish on the grill grate & cook for around 60 minutes.
- Serve the dip with crackers or a sliced baguette.

1.11 Honey & Sage Skillet Cornbread

Preparation time: 10 minutes

Cooking time: 25 minutes

Servings: 6

Ingredients

- One cup all-purpose flour
- One cup + three tbsp yellow cornmeal
- One tbsp baking powder
- Half tsp baking soda
- Two tbsp granulated sugar
- Half tsp kosher salt
- Two tbsp fresh sage, minced
- One large egg, beaten
- One cup milk
- One can cream corn
- Half cup softened unsalted butter
- Butter, flaky salt & honey for serving

- Set the grill temperature to 400°F, then keep the lid closed for 15 minutes.
- Put one cup cornmeal, the flour, baking soda, baking powder, salt, minced sage & sugar. Mix well.
- In another bowl put the egg, creamed corn & milk. Stir well but don't beat too much.
- Fold the dry ingredients into the wet ones.
- Melt the butter in a cast iron skillet; sprinkle the skillet with the three reserved cornmeal tbsp. Pour the batter into the skillet & level it with a spatula.
- Put the skillet on the grill grate, close the lid & cook for around 25 minutes.
- Take it from the grill, let it rest for ten minutes & cut into wedges. Serve hot with honey, flaky salt & butter.

1.12 Spicy Fries with Smoky Ketchup

Preparation time: 10 minutes

Cooking time: 15 minutes

Servings: 4

Ingredients

Chipotle Ketchup

- Two cans chipotle peppers in adobo sauce
- One tbsp olive oil
- One tsp onion powder
- One tsp garlic powder
- One cup tomato ketchup
- One tbsp sugar
- One tbsp cumin
- One tbsp chili powder
- Juice from one lime

Main

- Six potatoes
- Two tbsp butter, melted

- One tbsp beef rub
- 4 tbsp fresh parsley, chopped

Steps

- Finely chop the chipotle peppers & put them in a bowl along with all the other smoky ketchup ingredients. Mix well & let ret rest in the fridge one hour to let the flavors blend.
- Set the grill temperature to 440°F, then keep the lid closed for 15 minutes.
- Cut the potatoes into thick strips; put them in a bowl along with the beef rub & melted butter. Toss thoroughly to coat well.
- Put the potato wedges on a parchment-lined cookie sheet & cook in the grill for around 10-15 minutes. Take the potatoes from the grill, sprinkle with parsley & serve it with the smoky ketchup.

1.13 Ultimate Nachos

Preparation time: 15 minutes

Cooking time: 15 minutes

Servings: 4

Ingredients

- One bag tortilla chips
- Half cup salsa
- One lb. kielbasa sausage, cooked
- One cup chicken breast, cooked
- One lb. tri-tip, cooked
- Four tbsp scallions, chopped
- One small jar jalapeños, sliced
- Four tbsp black olives, chopped
- Two cups cheddar cheese, shredded
- Half cup sour cream
- Half cup guacamole
- Four tbsp cilantro, chopped

Steps

- When ready to cook, set the grill temperature to 375°F, then keep the lid closed for 15 minutes.

- Lay the tortilla chips out uniformly on a big cooking tray. Sprinkle some salsa on the chips first, then the shredded chicken, sliced kielbasa sausage, & cubed tri-tip. Top with scallions, olives, jalapeños, & cheese.
- Put the tray onto your grill, close the lid & bake about 10-15 minutes, until the cheese has melted & the nachos are hot.
- Serve with guacamole, sour cream & chopped cilantro.

2.1 Grilled Asparagus & Spinach Salad

Preparation time: 10 minutes

Cooking time: 10 minutes

Servings: 8

Ingredients

- Half cup apple cider vinegar
- Half cup bourbon honey BBQ sauce
- Four tbsp veggie rub
- Half cup candied pecans
- Half cup feta cheese, crumbled
- Two bunches asparagus, trimmed
- Six tbsp olive oil
- One lb. baby spinach

Steps

- Prepare the salad dressing. Mix in a small bowl the vinegar & BBQ sauce.
- Set the grill temperature to 500°F, then keep the lid closed for 15 minutes.
- Season the asparagus with the veggie rub, & drizzle with olive oil. Arrange the asparagus on a cookie sheet & put it on the grill grate.

- Cook for around 10 minutes on the grill. When the asparagus is done, remove it from the pan.
- Arrange the baby spinach on a serving dish. Add the candied pecans, salad dressing & feta cheese, tossing well to mix. Place the hot asparagus on top of the salad & serve.

2.2 Grilled Sweet Potato Planks

Preparation time: 5 minutes

Cooking time: 20 minutes

Servings: 6

Ingredients

- One tsp salt
- Half tsp onion powder
- One tsp pepper
- Five large, sweet potatoes
- One tbsp olive oil

Steps

- Peel & wash the sweet potatoes & then cut into eighths lengthwise.
- Place them in a bowl with olive oil, pepper, onion powder & salt, tossing well to mix.
- Set the grill temperature to 500°F, then keep the lid closed for 15 minutes.
- Place the sweet potatoes straight on the grill grate.
- Once they have developed nice grill marks, lower the grill temperature & cook 20 more minutes, till fork tender. Serve.

2.3 Smoked Pickles

Preparation time: 15 minutes

Cooking time: 1 hour

Servings: 8

- Half cup kosher salt
- Half tsp pink peppercorns
- Half tsp coriander seeds
- Two cups white vinegar
- Four tbsp sugar
- One tsp mustard seeds
- One tsp black peppercorns
- Half tsp celery seeds
- Eight garlic cloves,
- Three tbsp veggie rub
- One bunch fresh dill, chopped
- One quart water
- Twelve small-sized cucumbers

Steps

- Set the grill temperature to 180°F, then keep the lid closed for 15 minutes.
- Mix the salt, celery seeds, coriander seeds, peppercorns, mustard seeds & garlic cloves on a baking sheet.
- Put the baking sheet straight on the grill grate, close the lid & smoke for about 90 minutes. Mix the spices occasionally.
- In a medium saucepan, bring the water & vinegar to a boil. Remove the pan from the heat & whisk in the smoked herbs, veggie rub & sugar. Mix well to dissolve the salt & then add the chopped fresh dill.
- Arrange the cucumbers in a plastic jar & pour the hot brine, fully covering them. Let cool before, then close the lid & store in the refrigerator.
- Pickles can be served in a few hours, but they will taste al lot better after a day or two.

2.4 Green Beans Skillet

Preparation time: 55 minutes

Cooking time: 25 minutes

Servings: 6

Ingredients

- One cup cheddar cheese, shredded
- Half stick butter
- One tsp Lawry's seasoned salt
- Pepper to taste
- One onion, chopped
- Two cans mushroom soup
- One can fried onions
- Half cup sliced mushrooms
- Four cans green beans

Steps

- Set the grill temperature to 375°F, then keep the lid closed for 15 minutes.
- In a cast iron skillet, melt the butter, then cook the onions & mushrooms, stirring till softened.
- Add the green beans & mushroom soup to the skillet.
- Season with the seasoned salt & pepper & top with fried onions & shredded cheddar. Place the skillet on the grill grate & close the lid.
- Cook for 25 minutes & serve.

2.5 Yams & Marshmallow Casserole

Preparation time: 10 minutes

Cooking time: 1 hour

Servings: 6

Ingredients

- One tsp black pepper
- One bag miniature marshmallow
- Five yams
- One tsp vanilla
- One tsp kosher salt
- Half stick butter
- Half cup brown sugar

Steps

- Set the grill temperature to 375°F, then keep the lid closed for 15 minutes.
- Pierce the yams' skin a few times with a fork & arrange them on a cookie sheet. Place the sheet on the grill grate, close the lid & roast for around 50 minutes, or till extremely softened.
- Melt the butter over medium heat in a deep cast iron skillet, then add the vanilla, butter, salt & pepper & mix well.
- Remove the yams from the grill, let cool a bit & peel the skin off. Cut the yams into cubes & place them in the skillet with the butter mix, stirring to combine.
- Top the sweet potatoes with one bag of marshmallows, put the skillet on the grill grates, close the lid & cook for 15 minutes or till the marshmallows are golden. Serve.

2.6 Grilled Mango Salad

Preparation time: 10 minutes

Cooking time: 10 minutes

Servings: 6

Ingredients

- Two ripe mangoes
- Half head green cabbage, shaved
- Half cup chopped cilantro
- One tsp chicken rub
- Half head red cabbage, shaved
- Two tbsp olive oil
- One tbsp brown sugar
- Zest of one lime
- One tbsp thai fish sauce
- Three tbsp lime juice

Steps

- Set the grill temperature to 450°F, then keep the lid closed for 15 minutes.
- Cut the mangoes in half & remove the pit & skin. Apply a thin coat of chicken rub to the halves.
- Cook the mangoes directly on the grill grate for 10 minutes, turning once. Remove from the grill, let cool a bit & slice into thin strips.
- Place the sliced mangoes with the cabbage & cilantro in a medium mixing bowl.
- To make the dressing, whisk together olive oil, brown sugar, fish sauce, lime juice, & lime zest in a small cup. Pour on the vegetables & toss to properly mix. Serve.

2.6 Creamy Herbs-Infused Mashed Potatoes

Preparation time: 20 minutes

Cooking time: 1 hour

Servings: 6

- Five lbs. potatoes
- One & half cups water
- Three sprigs fresh thyme, plus more for garnish
- Two sprigs fresh rosemary
- One pint heavy cream
- Six sage leaves
- Six whole black peppercorns
- Kosher salt, to taste
- Ground black pepper
- Two garlic cloves, peeled & chopped
- Two sticks unsalted butter, softened

Steps

- Set the grill temperature to 450°F, then keep the lid closed for 15 minutes.
- Wash & peel the potatoes. Cut them into one-inch cubes. Place the cubes in an oven safe dish with one & half cups water & cook in the grill for around one hour or till fork tender
- In an oven proof skillet mix add the herbs, peppercorns, cream & garlic. Put on the grill grate, close the lid, cover & cook for 15 minutes.
- Strain the cream to remove the herbs & garlic, then return it to a saucepan & keep it hot on the stove.
- Drain the potatoes in a bowl & mash with a potato ricer. Pour in 2/3 of the hot cream slowly, one stick of soft butter & a teaspoon of salt. Mix thoroughly. To achieve the required consistency, add more cream, salt & butter as needed. Serve hot.

2.7 Butter Roasted Green Beans

Preparation time: 5 minutes

Cooking time: 1 hour

Servings: 6

Ingredients

- Ground black pepper, to taste
- One & half lb. fresh green beans, trimmed
- Veggie rub, to taste
- Half cup butter, melted

Steps

- Set the grill temperature to 325°F, then keep the lid closed for 15 minutes.
- Arrange the green beans in a single layer on a cookie sheet & drizzle with the melted butter. Season the beans with veggie rub & black pepper.
- Roasted the beans for 1 hour, stirring each 20 minutes. The beans must be wilted, soft & slightly browned in spots. Transfer the beans to a serving bowl & serve immediately.

2.8 Roasted Parmesan Cauliflower

Preparation time: 20 minutes

Cooking time: 40 minutes

Servings: 4

Ingredients

- One head cauliflower, cut into florets
- One medium onion, sliced
- Salt to taste
- Black pepper to taste
- Four garlic cloves, chopped
- Four tbsp olive oil
- One tsp fresh thyme
- Half cup parmesan cheese, grated

Steps

- Set the grill temperature to 400°F, then keep the lid closed for 15 minutes.
- Combine the cauliflower, thyme, garlic, onion, olive oil, pepper & salt on a cookie sheet.

- Place the sheet on the grill grate & cook till cauliflower is tender but still firm, around 25 minutes.
- Sprinkle the cauliflower with parmesan cheese & cook for an additional 10 to 15 minutes until the parmesan gets golden & crispy. Serve.

2.9 Baked Potato Casserole

Preparation time: 20 minutes

Cooking time: 25 minutes

Servings: 6

Ingredients

- Three garlic cloves, chopped
- One cup parmesan cheese, grated
- Pepper & salt
- Two tbsp rosemary, chopped
- Six potatoes, thinly sliced
- Two sticks of butter, melted

Steps

- Set the grill temperature to 375°F, then keep the lid closed for 15 minutes.
- Peel & slice the potatoes. Keep the potato slices in a bowl of cold water so that they would not oxidize). Melt the butter in a small skillet, add the crumbled garlic & mix.
- Butter a 12-inch cast-iron pan & start layering the casserole. Alternate layers of potatoes, rosemary, parmesan, butter & garlic mix. Keep layering until the ingredients are over.
- Place the pan inside the grill, cover the lid & bake for 20 to 25 minutes or till the potatoes are completely cooked. In case the top of the casserole starts darkening before the potatoes are done, decrease the grill temperature to 325°F. Serve.

2.10 Winter Squash Gratin

Preparation time: 15 minutes

Cooking time: 45 minutes

Servings: 8

Ingredients

- Two cups heavy cream
- Three cups gruyere cheese, shredded
- Pepper & salt to taste
- Three potatoes, peeled & diced
- Four garlic cloves, chopped
- One acorn squash, peeled, seeded & dices
- One butternut squash peeled & dices
- Two tbsp butter

Steps

- Set the grill temperature to 375°F, then keep the lid closed for 15 minutes.
- Heat the cream in a small saucepan, stirring continuously, till it reaches a low simmer. Season with pepper, garlic, salt, & gruyere. Stir until all the cheese is completely melted.
- Melt 2 tbsp butter in a baking dish (9x13 inch). Combine butternut, acorn squash & potatoes in a big mixing bowl. Add the cheese sauce & mix well. Place the mixture in the buttered baking dish & place the dish on the grill grate. Close the lid.

- Cook for approximately 45 minutes, or until the vegetables are fork tender. Allow 10 minutes to cool before serving after removing from the grill.

2.11 Pan Roasted Root Vegetables

Preparation time: 15 minutes

Cooking time: 45 minutes

Servings: 6

Ingredients

- One bunch golden beets, trimmed
- One bunch red beets, trimmed
- One large yam, peeled
- One large red onion, peeled
- One butternut squash, seeded & peeled
- Three tbsp fresh thyme
- One cinnamon stick
- One large carrot, peeled
- Four garlic cloves, peeled
- Three tbsp olive oil
- Black pepper, to taste
- Salt, to taste
- Two tbsp honey

Steps

- Set the grill temperature to 450°F, then keep the lid closed for 15 minutes.
- Cut all the veggies into half-inch chunks. Toss the vegetables with olive oil, thyme leaves, garlic & the cinnamon stick in a big mixing bowl.
- Line a big baking dish with foil, spread the vegetables in a single layer on the baking dish & season to taste with pepper & salt.
- Roast the vegetables for around 45 min or till fork tender. Take the baking dish from the grill, drizzle honey on veggies, let cool a bit & serve.

2.12 Baked Sweet Potato Hash

Preparation time: 15 minutes

Cooking time: 40 minutes

Servings: 4

Ingredients

- One lb. sweet potatoes, peeled & diced
- Eight oz oyster mushrooms
- Half red onion, diced
- Two tbsp olive oil
- Two tbsp thyme leaves
- One pinch salt
- Two cloves garlic, chopped
- One tsp smoked paprika
- Four eggs
- Black pepper to taste
- Four tbsp goat cheese, crumbled
- Two tbsp parsley, chopped

Steps

- Set the grill temperature to 450°F, then keep the lid closed for 15 minutes. Place a wide cast iron or ovenproof skillet straight on the grill grate for preheating while the grill is heating up.
- Place in the skillet the sweet potatoes, onions, mushrooms & oil, along with a generous pinch of salt. Cook for 20 minutes, stirring once in a while to coat the vegetables in the oil.
- Add the chopped garlic, paprika, thyme leaves, & a sprinkle of ground black pepper. Close the grill lid & cook for another 10 minutes, till the potatoes are golden brown & the onions are tender.
- Dig four holes in the vegetables & crack an egg into each one. Cook for another 10 minutes on the grill or until egg whites are mostly set.
- Take the skillet from the grill & finish the dish topping with chopped parsley & crumbled goat cheese. Serve.

3.1 Greek Style Roasted Lamb Leg

Preparation time: 25 minutes

Cooking time: 2 hours

Servings: 8

Ingredients

- Kosher salt, to taste
- Black pepper, to taste
- One lamb leg, bone-in, around 7 lbs.
- Eight garlic cloves
- Four tbsp fresh rosemary
- Six tbsp olive oil
- One sprig fresh oregano
- Juice of two lemons

Steps

- Cut a series of small slits in the lamb leg with the help of a paring knife.
- Mince the oregano, garlic, & rosemary on a cutting board with a chef's knife. You can also use a small food processor. Fill each of the slots a small quantity of the garlic-herbs mix, pressing it into the meat with a spoon or your fingers.
- Rub lemon juice & olive oil all over the outside of the lamb leg. Wrap into cling film & refrigerate overnight.
- Remove the lamb from the fridge & set it aside to come to room temperature. Remove the cling film & season the lamb with pepper & salt.
- Place the lamb leg on a parchment lined roasting pan.
- Set the grill temperature to 450°F, then keep the lid closed for 15 minutes.
- Place the roasting pan on the grill grate & roast the lamb for around 30 minutes. Decrease the heat to 350°F & continue cooking till the internal temperature of the thickest portion of the meat reaches 130°F for medium-rare, around 90 more minutes. If you like your lamb well done, keep roasting until desired doneness.
- Place the lamb on the cutting board, cover loosely with aluminum foil & let rest for at least 15 minutes. Slice the lamb thinly on a diagonal & serve.

3.2 Bread & Herbs Roasted Lamb Rack

Preparation time: 15 minutes

Cooking time: 20 minutes

Servings: 4

Ingredients

- One tbsp salt
- One tsp sage, minced
- One tsp rosemary, minced
- One tsp black pepper
- One rack lamb, around 2 lbs. frenched
- Half cup yellow mustard
- One cup panko breadcrumbs
- One tbsp parsley, minced

Steps

- If your butcher has not previously done so, trim & clean the lamb.

- Apply mustard to the exterior of the rack & season with pepper & salt.
- Mix the breadcrumbs & minced herbs in a baking dish. Coat the lamb in the mixture.
- Set the grill temperature to 500°F, then keep the lid closed for 15 minutes.
- Place the rack directly on the grill grate bone side down, close the lid & cook for a minimum of 20 minutes, or till the internal temperature reaches 120°F
- Remove the lamb rack from the grill, cover loosely with aluminum foil & set it aside to rest for 5 to 10 minutes. Slice & serve.

3.3 Butterflied Lamb Leg

Preparation time: 10 minutes

Cooking time: 80 minutes

Servings: 8

Ingredients

- One leg of lamb, butterflied & boneless, around 5 lbs.
- One onion, sliced
- Zest & juice of one lemon
- 4 tbsp red wine vinegar
- One cup olive oil
- Two tsp rosemary, minced
- One tsp thyme
- One tsp salt
- Four garlic cloves, chopped
- One tsp black pepper

Steps

- Prepare the marinade. Squeeze the lemon juice into the mixing bowl, reserving the zest. Stir in the rosemary, red wine vinegar, thyme, garlic, pepper, & salt. Mix thoroughly until the salt crystals have dissolved. Add the oil & whisk again.
- Place the lamb in a big resealable plastic bag. Pour the marinade, add the onion & lemon rinds & massage the bag to evenly spread the herbs & marinade. Refrigerate overnight.
- Remove the lamb from the marinade & pat it dry with paper towels. Discard the marinade.
- Set the grill temperature to 500°F, then keep the lid closed for 15 minutes. Place the lamb fat-side down on the grill grate. For the medium-rare, grill for at least 30-40 minutes on each side or till the internal temperature reaches 135°F. Transfer the lamb on a chopping board, cover loosely with aluminum foil & let rest for 15 minutes. Slice thinly across the grain & serve.

3.4 Pickled Onions Lamb Burgers

Preparation time: 20 minutes

Cooking time: 10 minutes

Servings: 4

Ingredients

Pickled onions

- Half red onion, thinly sliced
- Six tbsp lime juice
- Half tsp kosher salt
- Half tsp brown sugar

Tzatziki Sauce

- One cup greek yogurt
- Two tbsp lemon juice
- One garlic clove, minced

- Half tsp kosher salt
- Two tbsp herbs of your choice, chopped

Main

- Half red onion, chopped
- One lb. lamb meat, ground
- One tomato, sliced
- Eight oz pork meat, ground
- Two tbsp fresh dill, minced
- Four garlic cloves, minced
- Three tbsp fresh mint, chopped
- Half tsp black pepper
- Six burger buns
- Three tbsp parsley, chopped
- One tbsp olive oil
- Half tsp ground cumin
- One tsp ground coriander
- Lettuce leaves

- Prepare the pickled onions: in a small size bowl, combine the lime juice, onion, salt, & sugar. Add the sliced onions, stir to mix, cover, & refrigerate for at least 2 hours.
- Prepare the tzatziki sauce. In a small bowl mix the yogurt, garlic, lemon juice, herbs & salt. Cover & refrigerate for at least 2 hours.
- Heat the olive oil in a small size skillet over medium heat. Stir fry until wilted, around 5 minutes.
- Prepare the burgers. Mix the lamb, parsley, pork, mint, coriander, dill, salt, pepper, cumin, stir fried onions & garlic in a large mixing bowl. Work the mixture with your hands, taking care not to overmix.
- Make 6 equal size balls out of the mixture. Form into patties & place on a baking sheet lined with parchment paper.
- Set the grill temperature to 500°F, then keep the lid closed for 15 minutes.
- Grill the burgers till well-browned, around 2 to 3 minutes each side for medium-rare, or 5 minutes each side for well cooked. Cut the buns & warm on the hot grill grate, cut side down.

- Let the burgers ret for 5 minutes on a plate earlier to serving.
- Arrange the burgers on the buns & top with a dollop of herbed sauce of yogurt & some pickled onions on top.
- Garnish with lettuce, sliced tomatoes & serve.

3.5 Herbs & Garlic Smoked Lamb Leg

- Lamb rub, to taste
- Rosemary sprigs, to taste
- Three tbsp fennel seeds, ground
- Five garlic cloves, sliced
- One leg of lamb, 6-8 lbs.

- Rub the lamb leg with ground fennel & lamb rub.
- Cut a series of small holes in the lamb leg with the help of a paring knife. Insert the rosemary & garlic slices each hole. Refrigerate uncovered overnight.
- Set the grill temperature to 180°F, then keep the lid closed for 15 minutes.
- Place the lamb roast on the grill grate & smoke the meat for 1 to 11/2 hours.

- Raise the grill temperature to 425°F roast the lamb leg till a golden-brown crust appears.
- Reduce the grill temperature to 325°F & continue cooking till the internal temperature reaches 125°F.
- Remove the lamb from the grill, cover it with aluminum foil, & let rest for 10-15 minutes. Slice the meat across the grain & serve.

3.6 Rosemary Lamb Rack

Preparation time: 10 minutes

Cooking time: 3 hours

Servings: 2

Ingredients

- One dozen baby potatoes
- Two rosemary springs
- One bunch asparagus, trimmed
- Two tbsp olive oil
- Salt & pepper, to taste
- Half cup butter
- One lamb rack, around one lb.

Steps

- Set the grill temperature to 225°F, then keep the lid closed for 15 minutes.
- With the help of a rounded knife, remove the thin membrane from the ribs' backside. Sprinkle olive oil & rosemary on both sides of the ribs.
- Arrange the potatoes in a large baking dish & coat in the butter. Place the baking dish on the grill grates.
- Put the rack of ribs straight on the grill grates, next to the potato bowl. Smoke for three hours or till the lamb internal temperature reaches 145°F. Add the asparagus to the potatoes dish during the last twenty minutes of smoking.
- Remove the rack from the grill, cover loosely with aluminum foil & let rest for 15 minutes. Cut the lamb rack into chops & serve with the asparagus & potatoes.

3.7 Citrus Lamb Chops

Preparation time: 15 minutes

Cooking time: 15 minutes

Servings: 4

Ingredients

- Two tbsp lamb rub
- Four garlic cloves, minced
- Four thick cut lamb chops, around two lbs.
- Juice from half lemon
- Juice from half lime
- Four tbsp olive oil
- Three tbsp orange juice
- Four tbsp red wine vinegar

Steps

- Combine all the ingredients except the meat in a mixing bowl, whisking thoroughly to combine. Place the lamb chops in a plastic resealable, pour the marinade & massage the bag to evenly spread the flavors. Let marinate in the fridge for 4 hours or overnight.
- Remove the meat from the bag & pat dry with paper towels. Discard the marinade.
- Set the grill temperature to 400°F, then keep the lid closed for 15 minutes. Grill the chops for at least 5-7 minutes on each side, then flip & grill for additional 5-7 minutes on the other side.
- Take the lamb chops off the grill, wrap them in aluminum foil & set them aside for 5 minutes before serving.

3.8 Chipotle Lamb

Preparation time: 30 minutes

Cooking time: 2 hours

Servings: 6

Ingredients

- Four tbsp lamb rub
- Two tbsp rosemary

- Two tbsp parsley, chopped
- One rack lamb ribs, around 3 lbs.
- Black pepper, to taste
- Two tbsp chipotle peppers powder
- Two tbsp sage, chopped
- Two tbsp thyme
- Six tbsp olive oil
- Three garlic cloves, chopped

Steps

- Coat the lamb ribs in 2 tbsp of olive oil & season with chipotle powder & black pepper. Refrigerate the lamb ribs for a minimum of 15 minutes before cooking.
- Set the grill temperature to 275°F, then keep the lid closed for 15 minutes.
- Prepare the wet rub. Combine sage, rosemary, parsley, thyme, lamb rub in a bowl with 4 tbsp of olive oil.
- Baste generously the lamb ribs with the dry rub.
- Arrange the lamb ribs on the grill grate & smoke them till they reach an internal temperature of 120-125°F.
- Raise the grill temperature to 425°F & sear the meat till it reaches an internal temperature of 135-145°F.
- Take the lamb rack off the grill, wrap in aluminum foil & set aside for 10 minutes. Slice the ribs & serve.

3.9 North-African Ground Lamb Kebabs

- One & half lb. ground lamb
- One small onion, chopped
- Two garlic cloves, chopped
- Three tbsp cilantro, chopped
- One tbsp mint, chopped
- One tbsp ground cumin
- Two tsp smoked paprika
- Salt, to taste
- One tsp ground coriander
- One pinch ground cinnamon
- Two pita breads, for serving

Steps

- Mix all the ingredients, except the pita bread, in a large mixing bowl. Knead the mixture with your hands & shape it into 2-inches balls. With wet hands, shape the meat in a loaf form, about 4-inches long. Cover the kebabs with cling film & refrigerate overnight.
- Set the grill temperature to 350°F, then keep the lid closed for 15 minutes.
- Place the kebabs directly on the grill grate & cook for around 30 minutes, turning once, until the internal temperature hits 160°F.
- When the kebabs are almost done, place the pita breads on the grill to warm.
- Arrange the kebabs on a serving platter along with the wedged pita bread & serve.

3.10 Smoked Lamb Leg with Tomatillo Salsa

- Six garlic cloves

- One lb. tomatillos
- One small onion, halved
- Five serrano chiles
- One tbsp capers
- Four tbsp cilantro, chopped
- Half tsp sugar
- Salt, to taste
- Pepper, to taste
- Two tbsp olive oil
- Juice from half lime
- One cup chicken stock
- One whole leg of lamb, boned & fat trimmed
- One head garlic, peeled
- Two tbsp rosemary, chopped

Steps

- Set the grill temperature to 500°F, then keep the lid closed for 15 minutes.
- Thread the six garlic cloves, unpeeled, on a wooden skewer. Arrange the garlic, onion halves cut side down, tomatillos & serrano chiles on the grill grates. Grill until the sides of the vegetables start to brown.
- Place the chiles in a plastic bag & steam for 15 minutes. Peel the chiles. Also peel the garlic cloves. Transfer the garlic, chiles, tomatillos & onion to a food processor's bowl. Add cilantro, sugar, salt to taste & mix until smooth.
- Preheat a cast iron pan on the grill grates. When hot, add the olive oil, the tomatillo mixture & cook until reduced. Add chicken stock, lime juice & cover. Continue cooking until furthermore reduced, about two cups. Remove from the heat, season to taste with salt, sugar & let cool.
- Lower the grill temperature to 180°F. Wash the lamb leg, pat fry with paper towels & cut holes with a paring knife. Stuff the holes with garlic cloves & season the meat with salt, pepper & chopped rosemary.
- Arrange the lamb leg in the middle of the grill grates & smoke for 30 minutes. Raise the temperature to 350°F & cook the lamb for around 90 minutes, until the internal temperature hits 130°F.
- Remove the lamb leg from the grill, cover with foil & let rest for 20 minutes. Carve the meat as desired & serve with the tomatillo salsa.

3.11 Red Wine Roasted Leg

Preparation time: 4 hours

Cooking time: 2 hours

Servings: 8

Ingredients

Main

- One whole leg of lamb, bone-in
- One garlic head, peeled & slivered
- Three tbsp rosemary, chopped
- Three tbsp thyme
- Two tbsp olive oil
- Salt & pepper, to taste

Red wine reduction

- One cup red wine
- One cup beef stock
- Three tbsp butter
- Salt & pepper, to taste

Steps

- Wash the lamb leg & pat dry with paper towels. Cut hole in the meat with a paring knife & stuff the holes with garlic slivers.
- Coat the lamb in oil & season with salt, pepper, rosemary & thyme. Cover with film & refrigerate overnight.
- Remove the lam from the fridge & arrange in on a roasting rack, over a wide roasting pan. Pour in the pan the wine & stock. Set the grill temperature to 425°F, then keep the lid closed for 15 minutes.
- Arrange the lamb on the pan directly onto the grill grates. Cook for 20 minutes, then lower the grill temperature to 350°. Continue cooking for about 80 minutes more, until the internal temperature hits 130°F in the thickest part. Remove the leg from the grill, loosely cover with aluminum foil & let rest. Prepare the red wine reduction.
- Transfer any dripping from the pan to a saucepan & reduce to desired consistency. Add the butter, salt & pepper to taste. Whisk thoroughly to combine.
- Carve the meat as desired & serve with the red wine reduction.

4.1 BBQ Beef Ribs

Preparation time: 10 minutes

Cooking time: 8 hours

Servings: 4

Ingredients

- One six-bones beef rib rack
- One cup beef rub
- Two cups beef stock

Steps

- Remove the membrane from the back of the ribs. Insert the point of a rounded knife under the membrane, then grab it with the help of a paper towel & rip it off the meat.
- Sprinkle generously both sides of the ribs with beef rub. Massage the meat to help the flavors penetrate. Cover with film & refrigerate for 2 hours.
- When ready to cook, set the grill temperature to 275°F, then keep the lid closed for 15 minutes. Arrange the ribs on the grill grate & close the lid.
- Every hour or so, mop the ribs with boof stock, to keep them moist. Smoke until tender, until the internal temperature hits 210°F.
- To speed the process up, when the ribs internal temperature hits 160°F, you can wrap the ribs in aluminum foil.
- Remove the ribs from the grill, let cool a bit, carve & serve.

4.2 Mandarin Smoked Meatloaf

Preparation time: 30 minutes

Cooking time: 1 hour

Servings: 6

Ingredients

- Two lbs. ground beef
- Twelve slices bacon
- One onion, chopped
- Six garlic cloves, chopped
- One red bell pepper, chopped
- One cup panko breadcrumbs
- Two large eggs
- Two tsp beef rub
- Half cup milk
- One tsp Worcestershire sauce
- Four tbsp cilantro, chopped
- Six tbsp mandarin sauce

Steps

- Slice the bacon strips & stir fry in a pan, until golden brown. Remove with a slotted spoon. Keep the bacon fat.
- Stir fry in the bacon fat the pepper, onion, & garlic, until wilted.
- In a big mixing bowl add the ground meat, breadcrumbs, chopped cilantro, eggs, Worcestershire sauce, beef rub, milk, mandarin sauce & the sauteed vegetables. Knead the mixture with your hands to help the flavors spread.
- Form a loaf, wrap in cling film & refrigerate overnight.
- When ready to cook, set the grill temperature to 225°F, then keep the lid closed for 15 minutes. Transfer the loaf to a baking pan & arrange the pan on the grill grate. Close the lid & cook for about 1 hour, until the internal temperature hits 160°F.

- Remove the meatloaf from the pan, wrap in aluminum foil & let rest for 20 minutes. Slice & serve.

4.3 Smoky Cheek Tacos

Preparation time: 20 minutes

Cooking time: 6 hours

Servings: 8

Ingredients

- Three lbs. beef cheeks, trimmed
- Three tbsp beef rub
- Two cups beef stock
- One garlic head
- One onion, quartered
- Twenty small corn tortillas
- One bunch cilantro
- Two spring onions, chopped
- Feta cheese, for serving
- Lime wedges, for serving

Steps

- Ask your butcher to trim all the fat off the beef cheeks or do it yourself. Your tacos will taste better.
- Sprinkle the meat with beef rub & massage to help the flavors spread. Let rest 15 minutes.
- When ready to cook, set the grill temperature to 275°F, then keep the lid closed for 15 minutes.
- Arrange the beef cheeks directly on the grill grate. Close the lid & smoke for 2 hours or more, until the core temperature hits 160°F.
- Place the cheeks in an ovenproof pan. Add the quartered onion & garlic head, then pour the beef stock. Try not to submerge completely the cheeks. Return the pan on the brill grates & cook for more 4-5 hours, flipping the cheeks once, until fork tender.
- Remove the pan from the grill, drain the cheeks from the liquid & slice them. Arrange slices of meat in the corn tortillas, top with onion, cilantro & feta cheese, drizzle with lime juice & serve.

4.4 Smoked Brisket

Preparation time: 15 minutes

Cooking time: 9 hours

Servings: 8

Ingredients

Rub

- Two tbsp garlic powder
- Two tbsp onion powder
- Two tbsp smoked paprika
- Two tsp chili powder
- Six tbsp kosher salt
- Six tbsp black pepper

Main

- One whole brisket, trimmed, 12-14 lbs.
- One & half cup beef stock

Steps

- When ready to cook, set the grill temperature to 225°F, then keep the lid closed for 15 minutes.
- Prepare the rub. In a small bowl mix kosher salt, chili powder, garlic powder, smoked paprika, onion powder & pepper.
- Apply generously the rub to both sides of the brisket. Massage the meat to help the flavors penetrate.
- Arrange the brisket directly on the grill grate fat side down. Cook for 5-6 hours, until the core temperature hits 160°F.

- Remove the brisket from the grill, wrap in double aluminum foil twice & pour the beef stock into the foil packet. Close the packet & return to the grill. Cook for another 3 hours, till the core temperature hits 205° F.
- Remove the packet from the brill, unwrap the foil, then put the meat aside to rest for about 15 minutes. Slice against the grain & serve.

4.5 Irish Corned Beef & Vegetables

Preparation time: 10 minutes

Cooking time: 7 hours

Servings: 6

Ingredients

- Four lbs. corned beef brisket
- One tbsp dark sugar
- One tbsp pickling spices
- Half onion, chopped
- Four garlic cloves, chopped
- One can Irish Stout beer
- Four carrots, peeled & sliced
- One lb. small potatoes, washed & halved
- Half cabbage head, sliced
- One tsp fresh thyme
- Chopped parsley, for garnish

Steps

- When ready to cook, set the grill temperature to 180°F, then keep the lid closed for 15 minutes.
- Arrange the beef brisket onto the grill grate, close the lid & smoke for 3 ours.
- Remove the brisket from the grill. Increase the grill temperature to 250°F & preheat for about 15 minutes, lid closed.
- In a large ovenproof pot or dutch even, combine the garlic cloves, corned beef, pickling spice, brown sugar, & onion.
- Pour the irish beer into the pot, cover tightly with aluminum fill, transfer the pot to the grill grates, close the lid & braise for 4-5 more hours, flipping the brisket once, till the meat is fork tender.

- In the last cooking hour add to the pot the sliced carrots, cabbage, potatoes, & thyme.
- Remove the pot from the grill, remove the foil & let rest for 10 minutes. Slice the meat as desired & serve with the braised vegetables, sprinkling with chopped parsley.

4.6 Tri-Tip Roast with Pico de Gallo

Preparation time: 15 minutes

Cooking time: 90 hours

Servings: 4

Ingredients

Main

- One onion, chopped
- Three garlic cloves, chopped
- One bunch thyme, chopped
- Four tbsp balsamic vinegar
- One tbsp onion powder
- One tbsp garlic powder
- One pinch cayenne pepper
- One pinch red pepper flakes
- Half cup olive oil
- Salt & pepper, to taste
- One beef tri-tip roast, around 2 lbs.

Pico de Gallo

- One red onion, diced
- One jalapeño pepper, diced
- Three tomatoes, diced
- One bunch cilantro, chopped
- Juice of two limes
- Salt & pepper, to taste

Steps

- In the large mixing bowl combine the marinade ingredients, whisking well to combine. Place the tri-tip roast in a big plastic resealable bag. Pour the marinade in the bag & refrigerate overnight, flipping the bag a couple of times.
- When ready to cook, set the grill temperature to 165°F, then keep the lid closed for 15 minutes.

- Remove the tri-tip from of the marinade & pat dry with paper towels. Discard the marinade. Season the roast with salt & pepper & let rest for 10 minutes.
- Transfer the tri-tip to the grill grates & smoke for 90 minutes.
- Prepare the pico de gallo. Just combine all the ingredients in a mixing bowl. Stir thoroughly to combine & set aside until ready to serve.
- Remove the tri-tip from the grill, raise the grill temperature to 500°F & preheat for 15 minutes, lid closed.
- Return the tri-tip to the grill & sear for about 10 minutes on each side, until the internal temperature hits 125°F.
- Remove the tri-tip from the grill, loosely cover with foil & let rest for 10 minutes. Slice the roast against the grain & serve with the pico de gallo.

4.7 Salt & Pepper Pot Roast

Preparation time: 10 minutes

Cooking time: 3 hours

Servings: 4

Ingredients

- Four lbs. chuck roast, cut into chunks
- Two onions, sliced
- Two tsp kosher salt
- Four tbsp olive oil
- Black pepper, to taste

Steps

- When ready to cook, set the grill temperature to 400°F, then keep the lid closed for 15 minutes. Arrange in a dutch oven half of the roast chunks, half of the onions, salt, pepper, & olive oil. Repeat with the leftover ingredients, making a second layer.
- Cover tightly the dutch oven & transfer to the grill grates. Cook for about 2-3 hours, until the meat gets fork tender. If the roast is boiling rather than simmering, lower the grill temperature to 350° F.
- Remove the dutch oven off the barbecue. Remove the lid, let the meat cool a bit then skim the fat from the surface. With a spoon. Serve the meat with pasta, rice or any side of your choice.

4.8 Coffee Crust Tenderloin

Preparation time: 5 minutes

Cooking time: 1 hours

Servings: 8

Ingredients

- One beef tenderloin, around 4 lbs.
- Two tbsp olive oil
- Two tbsp ground espresso coffee
- One tbsp dark sugar
- Two tsp ground coriander
- One pinch cayenne pepper
- Half tsp garlic powder
- Salt & pepper, to taste
- One tbsp lemon zest
- One tbsp chives, chopped

Steps

- Set the temperature to 425° F, then preheat about 15 minutes with the lid closed until ready to cook.
- Prepare the tenderloin. Remove the chain that runs through the tenderloin. Remove any traces of fat or silver skin. Tuck the tenderloin's thin end under itself & tie the roast with kitchen twine every 2 inches.
- In a small bowl combine the salt, lemon zest, espresso, sugar, spices, chives & black pepper. Stir well to mix.
- Coat the tenderloin in olive oil, spread that spice rub over it & massage to help the flavors penetrate.
- Place the tenderloin directly onto grill grates & cook for 45-50 minutes, until the core temperature hits 130°F.
- Remove the beef from the grill & cover with foil. Let rest for 15 minutes. The core temperature will increase to 135°F.
- Remove the twine, slice the tenderloin & serve with sides of your choice.

4.9 Smoked Beef Jerky

Preparation time: 30 minutes

Cooking time: 4 hours

Servings: 6

Ingredients

- One cup coconut aminos
- Half tbsp thai fish sauce
- One tbsp onion powder
- One tbsp garlic powder
- One tsp black pepper
- Half tsp cayenne pepper
- Three lbs. flank steak

Steps

- Prepare the marinade. Combine cayenne pepper, coconut aminos, black pepper, fish sauce, onion powder & garlic powder in a mixing bowl. Stir thoroughly to mix.
- Trim any fat or silver skin from the beef.
- With a sharp knife, thinly slice the meat against the grain.
- Transfer the sliced meat to a resealable plastic bag. Pour the marinade mix over the meat & massage the bag to help the flavors spread.
- Refrigerate overnight, flipping the bag once in a while.
- When ready to cook, set the grill temperature to 165°F, then keep the lid closed for 15 minutes.
- Take the beef out from this marinade, then discard the marinade.
- Arrange the beef slices onto your grill grate in a single layer.
- Smoke for 4-5 hours, until the beef jerky is crispy but still chewy & pliable when bent in half.
- Remove the beef from the grill & let cool for one hour on a cooling rack.
- Store the beef jerky for up to two weeks in a resealable plastic bag in the fridge.

4.10 Brined Smoked Brisket

Preparation time: 20 minutes

Cooking time: 7 hours

Servings: 6

Ingredients

- One brisket, around 6 lbs.
- One cup dark sugar
- Half cup kosher salt
- Four tbsp beef rub

Steps

- In six quarts of boiling water, dissolve the sugar & salt. Turn off the heat, add six cups of ice & let cool. Put the brisket into the brine, cover & refrigerate for at least 24 hours.
- Remove the brisket from the brine & pat dry with paper towels. Discard the brine. Sprinkle generously with beef rub, massaging the meat to help the flavors penetrate.
- When ready to cook, set the grill temperature to 250°F, then keep the lid closed for 15 minutes.
- Arrange the brisket directly over the grill grates, fat side down, & smoke for around 3 hours.
- Raise the grill temperature to 275°. Wrap the brisket in double foil & cook for 3-4 hours more, until the core temperature hits 204°F.
- Remove the foil & put back the brisket into the grill for another 30 minutes.
- Remove from the grill, let rest for 15 minutes, slice across the grain & serve.

4.11 Blue Cheese Butter Steaks

Preparation time: 10 minutes

Cooking time: 40 minutes

Servings: 4

Ingredients

- Half cup butter, softened
- Four tbsp blue cheese, crumbled
- One clove garlic, chopped
- One tbsp red wine
- One tsp black pepper, coarsely ground
- One tsp coarse Salt
- One tbsp chives, chopped
- Four tenderloin steaks
- Two tbsp olive oil
- Two tbsp beef rub

Steps

- Prepare the blue cheese butter. In a bowl add the wine, butter, garlic, blue cheese, pepper, chives, & salt. Roll into a log in parchment paper & refrigerate until ready to serve.
- When ready to cook, set the grill temperature to 250°F, then keep the lid closed for 15 minutes.
- Brush the steaks with olive oil & season with beef rub, massaging the meat to help the flavors penetrate.
- Arrange the steaks on the grill grate, close the lid & smoke for about 30 minutes.
- Remove the steaks from the grill. Increase the temperature to 500°F, then preheat for 15 minutes with the lid closed.

- Return the steaks to the grill grate, then grill until desired doneness, turning once. The core temperature should hit 130°F for medium-rare.
- Serve the steaks topping with dollops of blue cheese butter.

4.12 Rosemary Prime Rib

Preparation time: 10 minutes

Cooking time: 1 hour

Servings: 8

Ingredients

- One rib-eye roast, about 8 lbs.
- Four tbsp olive oil
- Four tbsp peppercorns
- Four whole rosemary sprigs
- Four thyme sprigs
- Half cup garlic, chopped
- Half cup smoked salt

Steps

- When ready to cook, set the grill temperature to 500°F, then keep the lid closed for 15 minutes.
- Cut the rib eye roast in half. Coat both halves in olive oil, arrange on the grill grates & sear until dark golden. Remove from the grill.
- Place the peppercorns in a plastic bag & crush them with a rolling pin.
- Take the leaves from the sprigs of rosemary & thyme. Combine salt, broken peppercorns, rosemary, thyme, & garlic in a bowl.
- Coat again the rib eye halves with olive oil & rub with the salt blend, massaging the meat to help the flavors penetrate.
- Return the meat to the grill & roast for 20 minutes, then decrease the temperature to 300°F & cook for about 30-40 minutes, until the core temperature hits 125°F for medium/rare.
- Remove the meat from the grill, cover with foil & let rest for about 20 minutes. Carve & serve with sides of your choice.

5.1 Tandoori Chicken Wings

Preparation time: 30 minutes

Cooking time: 50 minutes

Servings: 4

Ingredients

Main

- Half cup yogurt
- One whole scallion, chopped
- One tbsp cilantro, chopped
- Two tsp ginger, chopped
- One tsp garam masala
- One & half tsp salt
- One tsp black pepper
- One & half lbs. chicken wings

Sauce

- Two tbsp mayonnaise
- Two tbsp cucumber, chopped
- Two tsp lemon juice
- Half tsp cumin
- One pinch cayenne pepper

Steps

- Combine in a blender the milk, cilantro, scallions, garam masala, ginger, pepper & salt. Process until smooth. Place the wings in a resealable bag, pour the sauce into the bag & massage to help the flavors spread. Refrigerate overnight.
- When ready to cook, set the grill temperature to 350°F, then keep the lid closed for 15 minutes.
- Remove the wings from the bag & discard the marinade. Place the wings onto the grill plate in an even layer. Cook for 40-50 minutes, until the meat is fully cooked & the skin is browned & crispy. Turn the wings once.
- Meanwhile, whisk together all of the sauce items; set aside & chill until ready to serve.
- Transfer the wings to a serving platter, drizzle with sauce & serve.

5.2 Oktoberfest Pretzel Mustard Chicken

Preparation time: 15 minutes

Cooking time: 25 minutes

Servings: 4

Ingredients

- 4 oz pretzel sticks
- Three tbsp Dijon mustard
- Three tbsp apple cider
- One tbsp honey
- Two tbsp fresh thyme, plus more for garnish
- Four chicken breasts, skinless

Steps

- Grind the pretzel sticks in a spice grinder or crumble them by hand in a zip lock pack until they are the consistency of panko breadcrumbs.
- Place the crumbs in a shallow, broad bowl.
- Whisk apple cider, mustard, sugar & thyme in another bowl.
- Place a wire rack on top of a sheet tray. Place chicken breast on the wire rack after dipping it in the mixture & dredging it in pretzel crumbs to cover evenly.

- When ready to cook, set the grill temperature to 370°F, then keep the lid closed for 15 minutes.
- Transfer the sheet tray on the grill grates & bake for 20-25 minutes, till the chicken breasts are completely cooked & the internal temperature hits 165°F.
- Let rest the chicken for 5 minutes, garnish with thyme & serve.

5.3 Asian BBQ Chicken

Preparation time: 1 day

Cooking time: 1 hour

Servings: 4

Ingredients

- One whole chicken
- Chicken rub, as needed
- One ginger ale can

Steps

- Clean the chicken by rinsing it in cool water & patting it dry with paper towels. Apply chicken rub all over the chicken, making sure to have plenty on the inside as well. Cover & refrigerate for 24 hours in a big resealable bag.
- When ready to cook, set the grill temperature to 375°F, then keep the lid closed for 15 minutes.
- Remove one fourth of ginger ale from the can. Place the soda can on a straight surface. Remove the chicken from the refrigerator & put it on the top of the soda can. To keep the chicken straight, the bottom of the can & the chicken legs must shape a tripod.
- Transfer the chicken in the middle of the grill grates & cook for 40 minutes to 1 hour, until the skin turns golden brown & the internal temperature of the chicken breast hits 165°F.
- Remove the chicken from the grill. Wearing a glove, carefully remove the soda can. Carve the chicken as desired & serve.

5.4 Grilled Chicken Alfredo Pizza

Preparation time: 15 minutes

Cooking time: 45 minutes

Servings: 4

Ingredients

- Two whole chicken breasts, skinless
- Chicken rub, as needed
- Eight tbsp butter
- Two garlic cloves, chopped
- Two cups heavy cream
- Half cup parmesan cheese, grated
- Half tsp black pepper
- One pinch nutmeg
- Two whole pizza doughs, cooked
- Two bell peppers, sliced
- Two cups mozzarella cheese, shredded
- Two tsp dried basil

Steps

- When ready to cook, set the grill temperature to 400°F, then keep the lid closed for 15 minutes.
- Generously sprinkle chicken rub on the chicken breasts. Massage the meat to help the flavors penetrate. Transfer the chicken to the grill grate & cook for 15 - 20 minutes, rotating once, until the internal temperature hits 165°F.
- Remove the chicken from the grill, allow them to cool slightly before cutting into cubes.
- Prepare the Alfredo sauce. In a medium saucepan over medium heat, melt the butter. Cook for 3 minutes after adding the

garlic. Add the cream & cook for 10 minutes, or until the sauce has thickened. Add the parmesan, nutmeg & pepper. Simmer for a few minutes more if the sauce is too thin.

- Arrange the pizzas on a baking sheet. Spread Alfredo sauce on top of each pizza crust. Divide the cubed chicken & sliced peppers between the pizzas. Top with shredded mozzarella & dried basil.
- Bake the pizzas for 10-12 minutes on the grill grate. Let cool for a few minutes. Cut into slices & serve.

5.5 BBQ Half Chickens

Preparation time: 15 minutes

Cooking time: 1 hour

Servings: 2

Ingredients

- One fresh young chicken, around 3 lbs.
- Chicken rub, as needed
- Four tbsp apricot BBQ sauce

Steps

- Place the chicken on a cutting board, breast side down, with the neck facing apart from you. Cut down the backbone from one side, remaining as near to a bone as possible. Repeat on the other backbone side, remove the backbone & discard it.
- Slice into the white cartilage at the top of the chicken's breastbone to crack it open. Cut either side of the breastbone & take it out of your fingertips. Break down the middle of the chicken, cutting it in two. Turn the chicken over, so the skin side is up.
- Generously season both sides of the chicken with rub, massaging the meat to help flavors penetrate.
- When ready to cook, set the grill temperature to 375°F, then keep the lid closed for 15 minutes.
- Place the chicken skin side up on the grill grate & cook for 60-90 minutes, until the internal breast temperature hits 160°F.
- Spread the BBQ sauce on the skin of the chicken & cook for another 10 minutes. Remove the chicken from the grill & let cool

for 5 minutes. Carve the chicken as desired & serve.

5.6 BBQ Chicken Breasts

Preparation time: 20 minutes

Cooking time: 30 minutes

Servings: 4

Ingredients

- Four whole chicken breasts, skin on
- Four tbsp olive oil
- One tsp garlic, chopped
- One tbsp Worcestershire sauce
- Two tbsp chicken rub.
- One cup BBQ sauce

Steps

- Combine the olive oil, Worcestershire sauce, garlic & rub in a small mixing bowl. Apply the mixture to the chicken breasts. Massage the meat to help the flavors penetrate.
- When ready to cook, set the grill temperature to 500°F, then keep the lid closed for 15 minutes.
- Arrange the chicken on the grill grate skin side down & cook for 20-30 minutes, turning once, until the thickest part of the breast hits 160°F. Glaze the chicken skin with BBQ sauce & cook for 10 more minutes.
- Remove the chicken breast from the grill & let cool for 5 minutes. Cut as desired & serve.

5.7 Lemon Chicken Breast

Preparation time: 5 minutes

Cooking time: 15 minutes

Servings: 6

Ingredients

Marinade

- One garlic clove, chopped
- Two tsp honey
- Two tsp kosher salt
- One tsp black pepper

- Two sprigs fresh thyme
- Zest & juice of one lemon
- Half cup olive oil

Main

- Six (6 oz) chicken breasts, skinless
- One lemon, wedged, for serving

Steps

- Prepare the marinade. In a small bowl mix the garlic, honey, thyme, salt, lemon juice, pepper & zest. Whisk until salt & honey are fully dissolved. Add oil in a steady stream & mix again.
- Put the chicken breasts in a big resealable bag. Pour the marinade over the chicken & massage the bag to uniformly spread the marinade.
- Set aside for 4 hours in the refrigerator.
- When ready to cook, set the grill temperature to 500°F, then keep the lid closed for 15 minutes.
- Remove the chicken breasts from the marinade & pat dry with paper towels. Discard the marinade.
- Transfer the chicken breasts on the grill grate & grill till the internal temperature hits 165°F.
- Also grill the lemon wedges alongside the chicken.
- Arrange the chicken & lemon wedges on a dish & serve.

5.8 Roasted Teriyaki Wings

Preparation time: 4 hours

Cooking time: 1 hour

Servings: 6

Ingredients

- 3 lbs. large chicken wings
- Half cup soy sauce
- Four tbsp water
- Four tbsp dark sugar
- Two tbsp. rice vinegar
- Two scallions, chopped
- One garlic clove, chopped
- Two tsp sesame oil
- Two tbsp fresh ginger, chopped
- One tbsp toasted sesame seeds

Steps

- Cut the wings from the joints to make three sections. Save the wingtips for making chicken stock or discard them.
- Place the drumettes & flats in a big zip lock bag.
- Prepare the marinade. In a saucepan mix soy sauce, water, vinegar, dark sugar, garlic, scallions & ginger. Bring to a simmer, then reduce the heat to low & continue to cook for 10 minutes.
- Let the marinade cool, then pour on chicken wings in the plastic bag.
- Refrigerate the wings overnight, turning the bag occasionally.
- Remove the wings from the marinade & pat dry with paper towels. Discard the marinade
- When ready to cook, set the grill temperature to 350°F, then keep the lid closed for 15 minutes.
- Transfer the wings to the grill grate & cook for 40-50 minutes, until the skin is golden brown & crispy, turning once.
- To serve, arrange the wings on a platter & top with sesame seeds.

5.9 Honey Lime Chicken Adobo Skewers

Preparation time: 15 minutes

Cooking time: 15 minutes

Servings: 6

- Four chicken breasts, diced
- One tbsp vegetable oil
- Two tsp garlic, chopped
- Two tsp onion powder
- Three quarters cup rice vinegar
- Four tbsp soy sauce
- Three tbsp honey
- Juice of two limes
- Salt, to taste
- Black pepper, to taste
- Lime wedges, for garnish

- In a big mixing bowl, combine all the ingredients, including chicken.
- Cover the bowl with cling film & refrigerate overnight.
- When ready to cook, set the grill temperature to 500°F, then keep the lid closed for 15 minutes.
- Remove the chicken cubes from the marinade & pat dry with paper towels. Discard the marinade
- Skewer the marinated chicken & cook on the grill grate, rotating occasionally, until done. It will take 12-15 minutes.
- Transfer the skewers to a serving dish, garnish with lime wedges & serve.

5.10 Baked Cranberry Chicken

Preparation time: 15 minutes

Cooking time: 1 hour

Servings: 6

Ingredients

- Six chicken breasts
- Four tbsp butter
- Half tsp salt
- One pinch black pepper
- Half cup onion, chopped
- Half cup celery, chopped
- One 6 oz can whole cranberry sauce
- One cup BBQ Sauce

- Season the chicken with pepper & salt. In a big skillet, melt butter & brown the chicken on both sides. Transfer the chicken breasts to a greased baking dish.
- In the chicken & butter drippings sauté celery & onion until wilted. Add the BBQ & cranberry sauces & cook for 2-3 more minutes, mixing thoroughly to combine. Pour the sauce over the chicken in an even layer.
- When ready to cook, set the grill temperature to 350°F, then keep the lid closed for 15 minutes.
- Bake for hour, until the chicken breasts are done. Occasionally spoon the sauce over the meat.
- Transfer the chicken breasts on a serving dish & drizzle with the pan drippings. Serve.

5.11 Spicy Grilled Chicken Thighs

Preparation time: 15 minutes

Cooking time: 25 minutes

Servings: 2

Ingredients

- Chicken rub, to taste
- Ancho chile powder, to taste
- Black pepper, to taste
- Four whole chicken thighs
- Four tbsp olive oil
- Two Garlic cloves, chopped
- Half Onion, chopped
- One jalapeño, chopped
- One pinch salt
- Half cup water
- One 14 oz can San Marzano tomatoes, crushed
- Two tbsp capers
- Half cup parsley, chopped

Steps

- When ready to cook, set the grill temperature to 500°F, then keep the lid closed for 15 minutes. Preheat a dutch oven or a large cast-iron skillet on the grill.

- Season each chicken thigh on both sides with chicken rub, black pepper & ancho chili powder. Transfer the thighs on the grill grate & cook 5 minutes each side.
- When the chicken is grilling, add the olive oil, garlic, jalapeno, onion, & a pinch of salt to the pan & cook for about 2-3 minutes until wilted.
- Deglaze the pan with half cup water, scraping the drippings from the pan with the help of a wooden spoon. Cook for another 5 minutes, until the liquid has been reduced by half.
- Add the chicken thighs, tomatoes with juice, capers & cook for 5 more minutes, or till the sauce thickened & the chicken is done.
- Stir in the parsley after removing the pan from heat. Serve.

5.12 Kansas City Spicy Fried Chicken

Preparation time: 1 hour

Cooking time: 25 minutes

Servings: 4

Ingredients

- One whole chicken, cut into pieces
- One & half cup buttermilk
- Two tbsp hot sauce
- Three cups all-purpose flour
- One tsp salt
- Half tsp black pepper
- One tbsp red pepper flakes
- Twelve oz bacon, chopped
- Vegetable oil, as needed

Steps

- When ready to cook, set the grill temperature to 180°F, then keep the lid closed for 15 minutes.
- Transfer the chicken pieces to the grill grate & smoke for 10 minutes.
- In a big mixing bowl combine buttermilk & hot sauce. Refrigerate.
- Combine the flour, salt, black pepper, red pepper flakes & bacon in another bowl & set aside.
- Remove the chicken from the grill & place it in the cold buttermilk mix, tossing well to coat. Refrigerate for around an hour.
- In a frying pan heat the oil to 370°F.
- Extract the chicken from the buttermilk & toss it in the dry ingredients mixture before frying it for 10-15 minutes. Serve with sides of your choice.

6.1 Kentucky Grilled Pork Tenderloin

Preparation time: 10 minutes

Cooking time: 15 minutes

Servings: 2

Ingredients

- One lb. pork tenderloin
- Four tbsp apple juice
- Four tbsp Kentucky bourbon whisky
- Four tbsp soy sauce
- Four tbsp dark sugar
- Two tsp Dijon mustard
- Two tsp Worcestershire sauce
- One tsp black pepper
- One onion, chopped
- Two garlic cloves, chopped

Steps

- Use a sharp knife to remove any fat or silver skin from the tenderloin. Place the meat into a big resealable bag.
- Prepare marinade. Whisk together the whisky, apple juice, soy sauce, dark sugar, mustard, Worcestershire sauce, & pepper in a mixing bowl. Add the chopped onion & garlic. Pour the marinade over the tenderloin, close the bag & refrigerate overnight

- When ready to cook, set the grill temperature to 400°F, then keep the lid closed for 15 minutes.
- Remove the pork tenderloin from the marinade & pat dry with paper towels. Discard the marinade.
- Arrange the tenderloin on the grill grate & cook for 6 to 8 minutes per side, until the internal temperature reaches 160°F for well done.
- Transfer the tenderloin to a chopping board, cover loosely with foil & let rest for 10 minutes. Slice into half-inch slices on a diagonal & serve.

6.2 Cider Glazed Holiday Ham

Preparation time: 15 minutes

Cooking time: 2 hours

Servings: 6

Ingredients

- Three apples, cored & thickly sliced
- One large ham
- Four cups apple cider, divided
- Four tbsp bourbon whisky
- Four tbsp Dijon mustard
- Four tbsp maple syrup
- Half tsp ground cinnamon
- One pinch ground cloves
- One pinch ground nutmeg

Steps

- When ready to cook, set the grill temperature to 325°F, then keep the lid closed for 15 minutes.
- Line a roasting pan with heavy-duty foil. To make a natural roasting rack, arrange apple slices at the bottom of the pan & place the ham on top of the slices. Pour one cup of cider.
- Transfer the roasting pan to the grill grates & bake for one hour & half.

- Prepare the glaze. In a shallow saucepan, mix the remaining 3 cups of apple cider & bourbon whisky. Bring to a boil over medium-high heat. Lower the heat & simmer until the liquid has been reduced by one-third. Add the garlic, nutmeg, cinnamon, mustard, & maple syrup, whisking to combine.
- As the ham is cooking, glaze occasionally with cider mixture, keeping any leftover for serving. Go on cooking for another 30 minutes, until the internal temperature hits 140°F.
- Remove the ham from the grill, cover with foil & let rest for 20 minutes.
- Slice the ham as desired & serve along with the warmed leftover glaze.

6.3 Pork Loin with Mango Salsa

Preparation time: 30 minutes

Cooking time: 40 minutes

Servings: 6

Ingredients

Rub

- One tsp chili powder
- One tsp garlic powder
- Half tsp onion powder
- 1 tsp smoked paprika
- One pinch cayenne pepper
- Half tsp salt
- Half tsp black pepper

Main

- One pork loin, boneless, around 3 lbs.
- One cup pineapple, diced
- One cup mango, diced
- One cup strawberries, diced
- On tbsp cilantro, chopped
- Half tsp salt
- Half tsp pepper
- Half tsp garlic powder

Steps

- In a small bowl mix all the rub ingredients. Season the pork loin with the rub mixture, massage to help the flavors penetrate & set aside.
- Prepare the mango salsa. In another bowl mix the pineapple, mango, strawberries, cilantro, salt & pepper. Stir thoroughly to combine.
- When ready to cook, set the grill temperature to 450°F, then keep the lid closed for 15 minutes.
- Arrange the pork loin on the grill grates & grill for a few minutes on all sides, until seared all over. Reduce the heat to 350°F & cook until the internal temperature hits 150°F.
- Remove the port loin from the grill, cover with foil & left rest for 15 minutes. Cut into half-inch thick slices, top with the mango salsa & serve.

6.4 Cajun Broil

Preparation time: 30 minutes

Cooking time: 1 hour

Servings: 8

Ingredients

- Two tsp olive oil
- Two lbs. red potatoes
- Old Bay seasoning, to taste
- Six corn ears, sliced into thirds
- Two lbs. smoked kielbasa sausage
- Three lbs. large shrimp with tails
- Two tbsp butter

Steps

- When ready to cook, set the grill temperature to 450°F, then keep the lid closed for 15 minutes.
- Drizzle 1 tbsp olive oil over the potatoes, sprinkle with Old Bay seasoning & transfer directly on the grill grate. Cook for 20 minutes.
- Drizzle the remaining olive oil over the corn, sprinkle with Old Bay seasoning & transfer the corn along with the kielbasa on the grill grates, next to the potatoes. Cook for 15 minutes.
- Sprinkle Old Bay seasoning on the shrimps. Transfer on the grill grates, alongside the

other ingredients & cook for 10 minutes, till bright pink & cooked through.

- Transfer all the cooked ingredients to a big bowl, add the butter & more Old Bay seasoning. Toss to coat & serve hot.

6.5 Smoked Pork Tenderloin

Preparation time: 5 minutes

Cooking time: 3 hours

Servings: 4

Ingredients

- Half cup apple juice
- Three tsp honey
- Three Tsp pork rub
- Four tsp dark sugar
- Two tsp thyme leaves
- Half tsp black pepper
- One pork tenderloin, around 2 lbs.

Steps

- With a sharp knife trim all the fat & silver skin off the tenderloin.
- Prepare the marinade. In a mixing bowl combine the honey, apple juice, pork rub, thyme leaves, dark sugar, & black pepper. Whisk thoroughly to combine.
- Place the pork in a big resealable bag. Pour the marinade over the pork, close the bag & refrigerate for 2-3 hours, turning the bag occasionally.
- When ready to cook, set the grill temperature to 225°F, then keep the lid closed for 15 minutes.
- Remove the tenderloin from the bag & pat dry with paper towels. Discard the marinade. Transfer the tenderloin straight on the grill grate & smoke for around 3 hours, until the core temperature hits 145°F.
- Transfer the tenderloin to a chopping board, cover with foil & let rest for 5 minutes. Slice as desired & serve with dishes of your choice.

6.6 Smoked BBQ Ribs

Preparation time: 25 minutes

Cooking time: 5 hours

Servings: 4

Ingredients

- Two St. Louis-style rib racks
- Four tbsp pork rub
- One cup apple juice
- BBQ sauce, as needed

Steps

- Remove the membrane from the back of the ribs with the help of paper towels. Pat the racks dry.
- Sprinkle the front, back, & sides of the ribs with an even coat of rub. Refrigerate for up to 4 hours.
- When ready to cook, set the grill temperature to 225°F, then keep the lid closed for 15 minutes.
- Transfer the ribs racks on the grill, bone side down. After 1 hour of smoking, fill a spray bottle with apple juice & spray the ribs. Spray the rib every 45 minutes.
- Check the core temperature of the ribs after four hours. When the core temperature of the ribs hits 200°F, they are done. If they are not done yet, smoke for 30 more minutes & try again.
- Spread a thin coating of your favorite BBQ Sauce on the ribs' top & back & cook for 10 more minutes, until the sauce to set. Remove the ribs from the grill, cover with foil & let rest for 10 minutes. Carve the ribs as desired & serve along with more BBQ sauce.

6.7 Teriyaki Pineapple & Pork Skewers

Preparation time: 3 hours

Cooking time: 10 minutes

Servings: 2

Ingredients

- One lb. pork sirloin, cubed
- Eighteen fresh pineapple pieces
- Six scallions
- Six wooden skewers
- One cup carne asada marinade

Steps

- Thread a pork cube, a chunk of pineapple, & a piece of green onion through the thin side of a skewer repeat the process, including 3 to 4 pork cubes per skewer. Repeat with the remaining skewers.
- Place the skewers in a big resealable bag, pour the marinade over the skewers, close the bag & refrigerate for 1 to 3 hours, occasionally turning the bag.
- When ready to cook, set the grill temperature to 500°F, then keep the lid closed for 15 minutes.
- Remove the skewers from the bag, pat dry with paper towels & discard the marinade. Transfer the skewers onto the grill grates & grill for 10 minutes, until the pork is cooked through, rotating once.
- Transfer the skewers to a serving dish & serve with steamed rice or any other sides of your choices.

6.8 Grilled Bacon-Wrapped Hot Dogs

Preparation time: 15 minutes

Cooking time: 20 minutes

Servings: 8

Ingredients

- Eight hot dogs
- Eight oz Cheddar cheese
- Eight slices of bacon
- Eight hot dog buns

Steps

- Cut the cheese into eight long pieces using a sharp knife. Cut the hot dogs lengthwise leaving a hinge on one side & stuff each with a slice of cheese.
- Wrap a strip of bacon around each hot dog in a loop & secure with toothpicks.
- When ready to cook, set the grill temperature to 350°F, then keep the lid closed for 15 minutes.
- Transfer the bacon-wrapped hot dogs on the grill grate & cook for 20 to 30 minutes, until the cheese melts & the bacon crisps up.
- Remove the hot dogs from the grill, arrange them into the buns & serve with your favorite sauces right away.

6.9 Apricot Pork Tenderloin

Preparation time: 5 minutes

Cooking time: 50 minutes

Servings: 4

Ingredients

- Two lbs. pork tenderloin
- Three tbsp pork rub
- One cup apricot BBQ sauce

Steps

- With a sharp knife, remove from the pork tenderloin any extra fat & silver skin. Generously sprinkle all over the tenderloin & let rest in the fridge for around 30 minutes.
- When ready to cook, set the grill temperature to 180°F, then keep the lid closed for 15 minutes. Transfer the pork tenderloin to the grill & smoke for 45 minutes.
- Remove the tenderloin from the grill, raise the grill temperature to 500°F & preheat for 15 minutes with the lid closed.
- Return the tenderloin to the grill grates & sear all sides of the pork tenderloin for

around 90 seconds, until the internal temperature hits 145°F.
- Spread the apricot BBQ sauce on the meat, let the glaze set for 5 minutes & remove the tenderloin from the grill. Cover with foil & let rest for 20 minutes. Slice the meat as desired & serve.

6.10 Pulled Pork Potato Skins

Preparation time: 15 minutes

Cooking time: 1 hour

Servings: 6

Ingredients

- Four large potatoes
- Olive oil, as needed
- Two tbsp butter, melted
- Four cups pulled pork
- Four tsp BBQ sauce
- One cup mozzarella cheese
- One cup cheddar cheese
- Salt, to taste
- Green onions for serving, chopped
- Cooked bacon for serving, chopped
- Sour cream, for serving

Steps

- When ready to cook, set the grill temperature to 450°F, then keep the lid closed for 15 minutes.
- Drizzle olive oil over the potatoes & sprinkle with salt. Arrange the potatoes straight on the grill grate & cook for 45 minutes, until fork tender in the center.
- Remove the potatoes from the grill, halve them & scoop out the insides, leaving 1/4 inch of potato skin on the outside. Place the skins on a baking tray & brush the insides with melted butter. Return to the grill & cook for 5-6 more minutes, until golden brown.
- Combine the BBQ sauce, pulled pork, mozzarella cheese & cheddar cheese in a mixing bowl.
- Stuff the potatoes skins with the mix & return to the grill. Cook, lid closed, until the cheese melts.

- Arrange the stuffed potato skins in a serving dish, top with green onions, bacon, & sour cream & serve.

6.11 Baked Supreme Pizza

Preparation time: 15 minutes

Cooking time: 30 minutes

Servings: 4

Ingredients

- One pizza dough
- Olive oil, to taste
- Half cup pizza sauce
- Two cups mozzarella cheese, shredded
- One tsp fresh oregano
- One handful fresh basil
- Parmesan cheese, to taste
- One lb. mild italian sausage
- Half green bell pepper, sliced
- Half red bell pepper, sliced
- Two tsp onion, diced
- Fresh mushrooms, to taste
- Sliced pepperoni, to taste
- Black olives, to taste

Steps

When ready to cook, set the grill temperature to 500°F, then keep the lid closed for 15 minutes.

Grease a 10-inches to 12-inches stainless-steel pan with olive oil. Cover the pan with the pizza dough & press it out through the bottom & up the edges.

Prepare the pizza. Spread the pizza sauce over the dough & top with italian sausage, green & red bell peppers, onion, mushrooms, pepperoni & black olives. Add the mozzarella, parmesan & sprinkle basil & oregano on top.

Transfer the pan to the grill grates & bake for 25-30 minutes, until the cheese & sauce are bubbling & the crust is golden brown.

Remove the pan from the grill. Let rest for 5 minutes, slice as desired & serve.

6.12 BBQ Bacon Bites

Preparation time: 10 minutes

Cooking time: 25 minutes

Servings: 2

Ingredients

- Half cup brown sugar
- One tsp ground fennel
- Two tsp kosher salt
- One tsp black pepper
- One lb. pork belly, diced

Steps

- Fold in half a 12-inches x 36-inches sheet of aluminum foil in half & crimp the corners to create a rim. Pin holes in the bottom of the foil with a fork. This will make some of the bacon fat drip, & the bacon bites will crunchier.
- When ready to cook, set the grill temperature to 350°F, then keep the lid closed for 15 minutes.
- Add the ground fennel, brown sugar, black pepper, & salt in a big mixing bowl. To mix thoroughly to combine.
- Throw the sliced pork belly in the mixture & toss until well coated. Transfer the pork bits on the double foil tin.
- Transfer onto the grill grate & cook for 20-30 minutes, until the bits are crunchy, golden & bubbly. Let cool a bit & serve.

7.1 Fried Halibut Sticks

Preparation time: 15 minutes

Cooking time: 20 minutes

Servings: 4

Ingredients

- Olive oil, as needed
- One lb. halibut
- Half cup all-purpose flour
- Half tsp salt
- One tsp black pepper
- Two large eggs
- Half cup panko breadcrumbs
- Two tbsp dried parsley
- One tsp fried dill

Steps

- Set the grill temperature to 500°F, then keep the lid closed for 15 minutes.
- Preheat on the grill grates a dutch oven with enough olive oil to fry the fish. It will take around 10 minutes
- Rinse & pat dry the fish fillets. Cut into 1-inch strips.
- Combine the salt, flour & pepper in the mixing bowl.
- Beat the eggs in a different bowl.
- Combine the parsley, panko breadcrumbs & dill in a third bowl.

- Dip the fish fillets in the flour, then in the eggs & finally the seasoned panko mixture.
- Fry the fish sticks in batches for 3-4 minutes, until done.
- Serve the halibut sticks with fries or any other side of your choice.

7.2 Tuna Burgers

Preparation time: 30 minutes

Cooking time: 15 minutes

Servings: 4

Ingredients

- Two lbs. fresh tuna, chopped
- Two eggs
- One tsp soy sauce
- One green bell pepper, finely diced
- One small onion, finely diced
- One tbsp fish rub
- Olive oil, as needed

Steps

- Combine eggs, tuna, soy sauce, green bell pepper, onion & fish rub in a mixing bowl.
- Lubricate your hands with olive oil & shape the fish patties.
- Set the grill temperature to 500°F, then keep the lid closed for 15 minutes.
- Transfer the patties close to the edges of the grill (the hottest spot) & cook for 10-15 minutes, flipping once.
- Remove the patties from the grill & serve with your favorite toppings.

7.3 Baked Salmon Cakes

Preparation time: 20 minutes

Cooking time: 1 hour

Servings: 4

Ingredients

- Two lbs. salmon fillets

- Salt, to taste
- Black pepper, to taste
- One small onion, diced
- One celery stalk, diced
- One red bell pepper, diced
- One tbsp fresh dill
- One tsp lemon zest
- Two tsp breadcrumbs
- Two large eggs
- Four tbsp olive oil

Steps

- Set the grill temperature to 275°F, then keep the lid closed for 15 minutes.
- Salt & pepper the salmon fillets & transfer them directly on the grill grate. Grill until the internal temp reaches 120°F. Remove the salmon fillets from the grill & set aside to cool.
- In a large mixing bowl, flake the cooled salmon fillets with a fork. Add the celery, onion, dill, bell pepper, lemon zest, eggs & breadcrumbs. Season with salt & pepper to taste & mix well to combine.
- Shape the salmon mixture into six 2-inches wide patties. Preheat the grill to 375°F, keeping the lid closed for 15 minutes. Inside the grill, preheat a cast iron skillet.
- Add olive oil to the skillet. When the oil is hot, Transfer the patties in batches to the skillet. Cook for 10-12 minutes, turning once, until golden brown on both sides. Serve the salmon cakes with sides of your choice.

7.4 Scallops & Shrimps Smoked Ceviche

Preparation time: 20 minutes

Cooking time: 1 hour

Servings: 4

Ingredients

- One lb. sea scallops, shucked
- One lb. shrimps, shelled & deveined
- One tbsp olive oil
- Juice & zest of one lime
- Juice of one lemon
- Juice of one orange
- One tsp garlic powder
- One tsp onion powder
- Two tsp salt
- Half tsp black pepper
- One avocado, diced
- Half red onion, diced
- One tbsp cilantro, chopped
- One pinch red pepper flakes

Steps

- Combine the scallops, shrimps & olive oil in a bowl.
- Set the grill temperature to 275°F, then keep the lid closed for 15 minutes.
- Transfer the shrimp & scallops on the grill grate & smoke for about 45 minutes. Combine all the other ingredients in a big mixing bowl while the seafood is smoking.
- Once the shrimp & scallops are done smoking, raise the temperature to 325°F & cook for an extra 5 minutes to ensure they are thoroughly cooked.
- Let the scallops & shrimp cool slightly before cutting them in half widthwise & combining them with the other ingredients in the dish.
- Refrigerate the ceviche for about 2-3 hours to allow the flavor to combine. Serve with corn chips.

7.5 Prosciutto Wrapped Shrimps with Peach Salsa

Preparation time: 20 minutes

Cooking time: 12 minutes

Ingredients

- Two lbs. shrimp, peeled & deveined
- Eight slices prosciutto ham, sliced lengthwise
- Two peaches, diced
- Two tbsp balsamic vinegar
- Two tbsp honey.
- One chile serrano, chopped
- One tbsp fresh basil, chopped
- Salt, to taste
- Black pepper, to taste

Steps

- Rinse the shrimps under cool running water & pat dry with paper towels. Wrap a strip of prosciutto across each shrimp & secure with a toothpick.
- Prepare the peach salsa. Combine peaches, honey, vinegar, chile serrano, basil, salt & pepper in a mixing bowl. Season to taste, adding more salt & pepper, if required.
- Set the grill temperature to 500°F, then keep the lid closed for 15 minutes.
- Transfer the prosciutto wrapped shrimps to the grill grate & cook it for 4-6 minutes on either side, until done.
- Toss the shrimps in the peach salsa & serve immediately.

7.6 Smoked Salmon Pizza

Preparation time: 15 minutes

Cooking time: 6 minutes

Servings: 4

Ingredients

- One pizza dough
- Four tbsp creme fraiche
- Four tbsp ricotta cheese
- Salt, to taste
- Black pepper, to taste
- Two tbsp chives, chopped
- Six oz smoked salmon
- One tbsp capers, drained
- Olive oil, as needed

Steps

- Set the grill temperature to 500°F, then keep the lid closed for 15 minutes.
- Roll out the pizza dough in the meantime.
- Transfer the dough on the grill grate directly. Cook for about 3 minutes per side.
- Remove the pizza crust from the grill & spread creme fraiche on top. Add the ricotta cheese & sprinkle with salt & pepper to taste.
- Arrange smoked salmon slices on top of the crust. Add chives & capers, drizzle olive oil on top & serve.

7.7 Teriyaki Salmon

Preparation time: 1 hour

Cooking time: 10 minutes

Servings: 2

Ingredients

- One cup soy sauce
- Six tbsp brown sugar
- Four garlic cloves, chopped
- One tbsp ginger, chopped
- Juice & zest of two oranges
- Four salmon fillets, about 6oz each
- One tbsp sesame seeds
- Chopped scallions, for serving
- Toasted sesame seeds, for serving

Steps

- In a saucepan, combine the soy sauce, brown sugar, garlic, ginger, orange juice &

zest. Bring to a boil & then reduce to a syrupy consistency, around a 50 % reduction. Let cool.

- Place the salmon fillets in a bowl & pour the reduced sauce. Refrigerate for one hour.
- Remove the salmon from the marinade & heat the marinade until it boils.
- Set the grill temperature to 500°F, then keep the lid closed for 15 minutes. Place the salmon fillets skin side up on the grill grate.
- Grill the salmon for 3-5 minutes on each side until cooked to your taste, occasionally brushing the salmon with the teriyaki sauce
- Remove the salmon fillets from the grill, transfer to a serving dish, top with sliced scallions & toasted sesame seeds & serve.

7.8 Baked Tuna Pasta Casserole

Preparation time: 30 minutes

Cooking time: 45 minutes

Servings: 4

Ingredients

- One 13.25 oz pasta box
- Two cups yogurt
- One cup almond milk
- One tsp ground mustard
- Half tsp celery salt
- One cup button mushrooms, sliced
- Ten oz cooked tuna
- One cup canned peas
- One cup cheddar cheese, shredded

Steps

- Bring a big pot of salted water to a boil over high heat. Cook the pasta according to the package instructions. Drain the water & set it aside.
- Combine almond milk, yogurt, ground mustard & celery salt in a big mixing bowl. Add the mushrooms, tuna, peas, cooked pasta & half of the cheddar cheese.
- Transfer the mixture into a greased 13" x 9" baking dish & sprinkle with the remaining cheddar cheese.

- Set the grill temperature to 350°F, then keep the lid closed for 15 minutes.
- Place the baking dish directly on the grill grate & cook for 45 minutes, or until cheese is melted & bubbly. Let cool 10 minutes & serve.

7.9 Lemon Butter Grilled Mussels

Preparation time: 50 minutes

Cooking time: 15 minutes

Servings: 4

Ingredients

- Two lbs. mussels, debearded & washed
- Five quarts water
- One third cup coarse salt
- Two garlic cloves, chopped
- One third cup white wine
- Juice of one lemon
- Three tbsp parsley, chopped
- One loaf french bread

Steps

- Set the grill temperature to 350°F, then keep the lid closed for 15 minutes.
- Scrub mussels thoroughly under running water to clear any mud & barnacles.
- Soak clean mussels for about 15 minutes in a wide bowl of 5 quarts of water & 1/3 cup coarse salt.
- Drain, clean & repeat the soaking process two or more times.

- In a frying pan, melt the butter. Add the garlic & cook for 1 minute, until fragrant. Add the wine, bring to a low simmer, add the mussels & the lemon juice.
- Transfer the pan to the grill & cover with a tight-fitting lid. Steam the mussels for 8-10 minutes. Remove the pan from the grill & discard the mussels that have not opened.
- Transfer the mussels to a serving dish, top with minced parsley & serve with sliced bread.

7.10 Mahi-Mahi Kebabs

Preparation time: 15 minutes

Cooking time: 8 minutes

Servings: 4

Ingredients

- One mahi-mahi fillet, around 2 lbs.
- One zucchini
- One red onion
- One cup baby carrots
- One cup flat green beans
- Half cup olive oil
- Two tsp fish rub
- One tbsp basil leaves, chopped

Steps

- Cut the mahi-mahi into chunks.
- Slice the zucchini, green beans, carrots. Cut the onion into squares. Combine all the ingredients in a mixing bowl, tossing to combine.
- Thread all the ingredients on 4 skewers, alternating.
- Set the grill temperature to 500°F, then keep the lid closed for 15 minutes.
- Transfer the kebabs on the grill grates & cook it for about 8 minutes, turning once. Serve with white rice or any side of your choice.

7.11 Baked Whole Fish in Sea Salt

Preparation time: 10 minutes

Cooking time: 30 minutes

Servings: 4

Ingredients

- Two sea basses, around 3 lbs. in total
- Ten thyme sprigs
- One lemon, thinly sliced
- Five cups coarse sea salt
- Ten egg whites
- Olive oil, for serving
- Lemon juice, for serving

Steps

- Set the grill temperature to 500°F, then keep the lid closed for 15 minutes.
- Cut the fish's gills & clip the fins. Stuff the fish cavity with lemon slices & thyme sprigs. Whip the egg whites to soft peaks & fold in the sea salt.
- Arrange the fish on a baking dish & cover with the egg-salt mixture.
- Place the dish directly on the grill & cook for about 30 minutes, until the internal temperature hits 140°F. Remove the pan from the grill & let cool for 10 minutes.
- With a wooden spoon, crack the crust open to clear any residual salt from the fish's skin.
- Remove the skin from the fish, drizzle with olive oil, lemon juice & serve.

7.12 Balsamic Grilled Salmon

Preparation time: 5 minutes

Cooking time: 25 minutes

Servings: 2

Ingredients

- One lb. salmon fillet
- One tbsp fish rub
- Half cup balsamic vinegar
- One tbsp garlic, chopped
- Two tbsp honey

Steps

- Generously sprinkle the fish rub all over the salmon, massaging to help the flavors penetrate.
- Prepare the glaze. Mix the garlic, vinegar & honey in a small pan. Simmer on medium fire until the liquid is reduced by half, & it coats the back of a spoon. Using a brush coat the salmon fillet in the glaze.
- Set the grill temperature to 350°F, then keep the lid closed for 15 minutes.
- Place the fillet of salmon directly on the grill grates. Grill the salmon for 25-30 minutes, until it gets opaque & easily flakes with a fork.
- Transfer to a serving dish & serve with sides of your choice.

8.1 Smoked Sangria

Preparation time: 10 minutes

Cooking time: 45 minutes

Servings: 6

Ingredients

- One bottle medium-bodied red wine
- Four tbsp Grand Marnier
- Four tbsp simple syrup
- One cup fresh cranberries
- One apple, sliced
- Two limes, sliced
- Four cinnamon sticks
- Soda water, as needed
- Ice, as needed

Steps

- Set the grill temperature to 180°F, then keep the lid closed for 15 minutes.
- Mix the simple syrup, cranberries, red wine, & Grand Marnier in a small ovenproof cup & place it directly on the grill grate.
- Smoke the liquid for around 30 minutes, until desired smokiness. Remove the cup from the grill & set aside to cool.
- Pour the mixture into a big pitcher. Add cinnamon sticks, sliced limes sliced apples & ice.
- Top with soda water to taste & serve.

8.2 Grilled Mango Coleslaw

Preparation time: 10 minutes

Cooking time: 10 minutes

Servings: 6

Ingredients

Main

- Two ripe mangoes
- One tbsp chicken rub
- Half head red cabbage, shaved
- Half head green cabbage, shaved
- Half cup cilantro, chopped

Dressing

- Two tbsp olive oil
- One tbsp soy sauce
- One tbsp lime juice
- One tbsp brown sugar
- Zest of one lime

Steps

- When ready to cook, set the grill temperature to 450°F, then keep the lid closed for 15 minutes.
- Cut the mangoes in half & remove the pit & skin. Apply a thin coat of chicken rub to the mangoes.
- Place the mangoes halves directly on the grill grates. Grill for 10 minutes, turning once. Remove the mangoes from the grill & thinly slice.
- Toss the sliced mangoes with the red & green cabbage in a big mixing bowl.
- Prepare the dressing. Whisk together olive oil, fish sauce, lime zest, brown sugar & lime juice in a small cup. Pour the dressing on the vegetable & mix thoroughly to combine.
- Transfer the slaw to a serving dish, top with chopped cilantro & serve.

8.3 Smoked Cinnamon Almonds

Preparation time: 5 minutes

Cooking time: 90 minutes

Servings: 4

Ingredients

- One egg white
- Half cup granulated sugar
- Half cup brown sugar
- One tbsp ground cinnamon
- One pinch salt
- One lb. unsalted almonds

Steps

- In a bowl whisk the egg white until frothy. Add the cinnamon, white sugar, brown sugar & salt. Toss the almonds in & mix well to coat.
- Arrange the almonds in a single layer on a cookie sheet lined with parchment paper.
- When ready to cook, set the grill temperature to 225°F, then keep the lid closed for 15 minutes.
- Transfer the cookie sheet to the grill grates & smoke the almonds for around 90 minutes, occasionally stirring, until the coating is completely dry.
- Remove from the grill, let cool for 10 minutes & serve.

8.4 Thyme & Rosemary Creamy Mashed Potatoes

Preparation time: 20 minutes

Cooking time: 1 hour

Servings: 6

Ingredients

- Five lbs. russet potatoes
- Half cup water
- One pint heavy cream
- Two sprigs fresh rosemary
- Three sprigs fresh thyme
- Six sage leaves
- Six whole black peppercorns
- Two cloves garlic, chopped
- Two sticks softened butter
- Kosher salt, to taste
- Black pepper, to taste

Steps

- When ready to cook, set the grill temperature to 350°F, then keep the lid closed for 15 minutes.
- Wash the potatoes & cut them into 1-inch cubes. Transfer to an oven-safe dish with half cup of water, place the dish on the grill grates & cook for 1 hour, until fork tender.
- In a saucepan combine the cream, sage, rosemary, thyme, garlic & peppercorns. Transfer to the grill grates, cover & cook for 15 minutes.
- Drain the cream, remove & discard the herbs & garlic, & then return it to a saucepan & keep it warm.
- Drain the potatoes & rice them in a big bowl with a potato ricer. Add 2/3 of the cream, one stick of butter & a teaspoon of salt. Mix thoroughly. To achieve the required consistency, add more cream, butter, & salt as required. Serve.

8.5 Fruit & Berries with Cream

Preparation time: 15 minutes

Cooking time: 10 minutes

Servings: 4

- Two peaches, halved
- Two apricots, halved
- One nectarine, halved
- Half cup balsamic vinegar
- Three tbsp honey
- One tbsp orange zest, chopped
- Two cups heavy cream
- Half cup fresh raspberries
- Four tbsp fresh blueberries

Steps

- When ready to cook, set the grill temperature to 400°F, then keep the lid closed for 15 minutes.
- Grill the apricots, nectarines, & peaches for 3 to 4 minutes on each side, until grill marks appear.
- Prepare the balsamic reduction. Combine the balsamic vinegar, 2 tbsp honey & the orange zest in a skillet. Bring to a boil & simmer until the sauce has thickened to a medium consistency.
- Meanwhile, whip the cream with the leftover 1 tbsp honey in a mixing bowl until soft peaks appear.
- Transfer the grilled fruits to a serving dish, top with the berries, drizzle with the balsamic reduction & serve along with the whipped cream.

8.6 Grilled Broccoli Rabe

Preparation time: 15 minutes

Cooking time: 10 minutes

Servings: 4

Ingredients

- Four tbsp olive oil
- Four bunches broccoli rabe
- Kosher salt, to taste
- Juice of half lemon

Steps

- When ready to cook, set the grill temperature to 450°F, then keep the lid closed for 15 minutes.

- Drizzle the olive oil over the broccoli rabe on a platter or in a mixing bowl. Mix thoroughly with your palms, evenly coating the vegetables. Season with a pinch of salt.
- Transfer the broccoli rabe to the grill grates, in a single layer. Cook for 5 to 10 minutes, until nicely colored & slightly charred.
- Place the broccoli rabe on a serving platter, drizzle with the juice of half a lemon & serve.

8.7 Smoked Deviled Eggs

Preparation time: 15 minutes

Cooking time: 30 minutes

Servings: 4

Ingredients

- Eight hard-boiled eggs, peeled
- Three tbsp mayonnaise
- Three tbsp chives, diced
- One tbsp french mustard
- One tbsp white wine vinegar
- Pepper & salt, to taste
- Hot sauce, to taste
- Smoked paprika, to taste

Steps

- When ready to cook, set the grill temperature to 180°F, then keep the lid closed for 15 minutes.
- Transfer the boiled eggs directly onto the grill grates & smoke for 30 minutes.
- Remove the eggs from the grill & set them aside to cool. Halve the eggs lengthwise, remove the yolks & place them into a mixing bowl.
- Add the chives, mayonnaise, salt, vinegar, hot sauce, mustard, & pepper. Mix thoroughly with a fork until combined.
- Spoon the mixture into the halved egg whites. Sprinkle with smoked paprika & serve or refrigerate until ready to serve.

8.8 Smoked Hummus with Vegetables

Preparation time: 15 minutes

Cooking time: 40 minutes

Servings: 4

Ingredients

- Half cup chickpeas, cooked
- Half cup tahini
- One tbsp garlic, chopped
- Six tbsp olive oil
- One tbsp salt
- Four tbsp lemon juice
- One red onion, sliced
- Two cups butternut squash, cubed
- Two cups cauliflower florets
- Two cups Brussels sprouts
- Two portobello mushrooms, cubed
- Salt, to taste
- Black pepper, to taste

Steps

- When ready to cook, set the grill temperature to 180°F, then keep the lid closed for 15 minutes.
- Prepare the smoked hummus. Rinse & drain the chickpeas, then lay them out on a sheet tray to create the hummus. Transfer the tray to the grill grates & smoke for 15-20 minutes, or until desired smokiness is achieved.
- Add lemon juice, salt, garlic, smoked chickpeas, olive oil & tahini to the bowl of a food processor & process until fully combined but not smooth. Set aside.
- Raise the grill temperature to 500°F, then keep the lid closed for 15 minutes to preheat.
- Place all the vegetables on a sheet tray & drizzle with olive oil. Transfer to the grill grates & roast for 15-20 minutes, until slightly charred & cooked to taste.
- Arrange the vegetables on a serving dish. Transfer the smoked hummus to a serving bowl. Drizzle the vegetables with more olive oil, season with salt & pepper to taste & serve with pita bread.

8.9 Garlic & Parmesan Grilled Corn Cobs

Preparation time: 5 minutes

Cooking time: 30 minutes

Servings: 6

Ingredients

- Four tbsp butter, melted
- Two garlic cloves, minced
- Six corn ears, husked
- Half cup parmesan, grated
- One tsp parsley, chopped
- Salt, to taste
- Pepper, to taste

Steps

- When ready to cook, set the grill temperature to 450°F, then keep the lid closed for 15 minutes.
- In a small bowl combine the butter, garlic, salt, & pepper.
- Rub half of the garlic butter paste on the corn cobs.
- Transfer the cobs directly on grill grate. Cook, regularly rotating, for 25-30 minutes, until corn is soft.
- Remove the corn from the grill & transfer to a serving dish. Top with the remaining butter mixture, sprinkle with parsley & serve.

8.10 Smoked Pico de Gallo

Preparation time: 10 minutes

Cooking time: 30 minutes

Servings: 4

Ingredients

- Three cups tomatoes, diced
- One jalapeño pepper, chopped
- Half red onion, diced
- Four tbsp cilantro, chopped
- Juice of two limes
- Four tbsp olive oil
- Salt, to taste
- Pepper, to taste

Steps

- When ready to cook, set the grill temperature to 180°F, then keep the lid closed for 15 minutes.
- Spread the tomatoes on a cookie sheet. Transfer to the grill grates & smoke for 30 minutes or until desired smokiness.
- Remove the tomatoes from the grill & let cook. Combine in a bowl with the jalapeño pepper, diced onion, chopped cilantro, lime juice & olive oil. Season with salt & pepper to taste & mix to combine. Serve with corn chips.

8.11 Brussel Sprouts Smoked Salad

Preparation time: 20 minutes

Cooking time: 30 minutes

Servings: 6

Ingredients

- One sweet potato, peeled & cubed
- Two parsnips, peeled & cubed
- Four shallots, sliced
- Four tbsp olive oil
- Two oranges, halved
- Four oz Feta cheese, crumbled
- Kosher salt, to taste
- Black pepper, to taste
- Two tbsp white wine vinegar
- One lb. Brussels sprouts, shaved
- Half cup pomegranate seeds
- Three tbsp fresh mint, chopped

Steps

- When ready to cook, set the grill temperature to 450°F, then keep the lid closed for 15 minutes.
- On a baking dish arrange the sweet potato, parsnips, shallots & 2 tbsp olive oil. Season with salt & pepper & toss to combine. Spread the vegetables in a single layer & cook for 30 minutes, until the vegetables are golden & crispy. Remove from the grill & let cool.
- While the vegetables are cooking, put the oranges cut side down on the grill & cook for around 15 minutes, until soft & slightly browned. Remove from the barbecue, chill, & strain the juice into a measuring cup.
- Prepare the vinaigrette. Combine the Feta cheese, five tbsp smoked orange juice & the vinegar in a blender or food processor & blend until smooth. Add the leftover 2 tbsp of oil & process again. Season to taste with salt & pepper.
- In a big bowl mix the shaved Brussels sprouts & roasted vegetables. Add the vinaigrette & toss to combine. Taste & season with more salt if necessary. Garnish with pomegranate seeds & mint leaves. Serve.

8.12 Sake & Thyme Baked Mushrooms

Preparation time: 15 minutes

Cooking time: 35 minutes

Servings: 4

Ingredients

- Four tbsp butter
- Two tbsp olive oil
- One shallot, chopped
- Two lbs. portobello mushrooms
- Salt, to taste
- Four tbsp sake
- One tbsp fresh thyme

Steps

- When ready to cook, set the grill temperature to 500°F, then keep the lid closed for 15 minutes.

- Place a big cast iron pan on the grill grates to preheat. Add the butter, close the lid & wait 5 minutes for the butter to melt.
- Add to the pan the olive oil shallot & salt to taste. Cook, covered, for 5 minutes, until the shallot has wilted.
- Trim the stems from the cleaned mushrooms before cleaning slice them. Add the mushrooms to the pan, close the lib & simmer for 15 minutes, stirring every 5 minutes.
- Stir in the sake & thyme, then cover the lid & simmer for 10 more minutes. Remove from the grill, let cool a bit & serve.

9.1 Amaretto & Ricotta Brownies

Preparation time: 5 minutes

Cooking time: 30 minutes

Servings: 4

Ingredients

- One cup ricotta cheese
- One egg
- One tbsp Amaretto liqueur
- Four tbsp sugar
- Two tsp cornstarch
- Half tsp vanilla extract
- One box brownie mix

Steps

- Line a 9x13-inches baking pan with parchment paper.
- In a mixing bowl whisk together the egg, Amaretto liqueur, cornstarch, sugar & vanilla.
- Prepare the brownie mix according to the box directions. Spread the brownie mixture uniformly in the baking pan. Drop dollops of ricotta mixture into the brownie mix. To realize a marbled pattern, move a knife through the mixture.

- When ready to cook, set the grill temperature to 350°F, then keep the lid closed for 15 minutes.
- Transfer the baking pan onto the grill grates & bake for 25 to 30 minutes. Check if the brownies are done sticking a bamboo skewer into the center: it should come out clean.
- Remove the pan from the grill & let cool completely. Cut the brownies into squares & serve.

9.2 Grilled S'more Croissants

Preparation time: 15 minutes

Cooking time: 2 minutes

Servings: 6

Ingredients

- Six croissants
- Twenty-five large marshmallows
- Eight oz chocolate

Steps

- When ready to cook, set the grill temperature to 500°F, then keep the lid closed for 15 minutes.
- Halve the croissants lengthwise & place them cut side down on the grill grates for one minute, taking care not to burn.
- Assemble the s'mores. Take the croissants from the grill & layer one half croissant, marshmallows, chocolate squares, & finish with the other half of the croissant.
- Toast the s'mores on the grill for up to 1 minute, until the chocolate has melted & the marshmallows have turned golden.
- Remove the s'mores from the grill, let cool a bit & serve while they are still warm & gooey.

9.3 Irish Cream Cake

Preparation time: 20 minutes

Cooking time: 1 hour

Ingredients

- One cup pecans, chopped
- One package yellow cake mix
- One package instant vanilla pudding
- Four eggs.
- Half cup olive oil
- One cup Irish Cream liquor
- Half cup butter
- One cup sugar

Steps

- Butter & flour a 10-inches baking dish. Spread the chopped pecans on the bottom of the dish.
- In a mixing bowl combine the pudding mix, yellow cake mixes, one quarter cup of water, eggs, oil & Irish Cream liquor. Blend with an electric mixer. Pour the mixture on top of the pecans, in the baking dish.
- When ready to cook, set the grill temperature to 325°F, then keep the lid closed for 15 minutes.
- Bake for 60 minutes, until a toothpick inserted in the middle of the cake comes out clean Remove from heat & set aside to cool for about 10 minutes.
- While the cake is cooling, bring to a boil in a small saucepan one quarter water, the butter & the sugar. Cook, stirring continuously, for 5 minutes. Remove the pan from the heat & stir in the Irish Cream liquor.
- Slowly pour the glaze over the cake. Allow the glaze to soak into the cake & serve.

9.4 Baked Banana Bread

Preparation time: 15 minutes

Cooking time: 1 hour

Servings: 4

Ingredients

- Two bananas
- Half cup brown sugar
- Half cup milk
- One tsp butter, for greasing
- One tbsp coconut oil
- One egg
- Two tsp vanilla extract
- Three quarters cup all-purpose flour
- Three quarters cup almond Flour
- One tsp baking powder
- One pinch kosher salt
- One tsp ground cinnamon
- Half cup dark chocolate chunks

Steps

When ready to cook, set the grill temperature to 350°F, then keep the lid closed for 15 minutes.

Grease with 1 tbsp of butter a 9 x 5-inches loaf pan.

Mash the bananas with a fork & transfer to a big mixing bowl. Add the brown sugar, coconut oil, milk, egg, & vanilla extract. Mix thoroughly to combine.

In another bowl, whisk together the baking powder, flour, salt & ground cinnamon.

Combine the wet & dry ingredients in the first mixing bowl & whisk until smooth. Fold in the dark chocolate chunks with a spatula until they are evenly distributed.

Pour the batter into the loaf pan, transfer to the grill grates & bake for 50-55 minutes, until a toothpick inserted in the center comes out clean.

Remove the loaf from the grill, let cool for ten minutes then place the banana bread onto a wire rack & let cool completely. Slice as desired & serve.

9.5 Carrot Cake with Cheese Frosting

Preparation time: 10 minutes

Cooking time: 30 minutes

Servings: 8

Ingredients

- To cups all-purpose flour
- Two tbsp baking soda

- One pinch salt
- Two tsp ground cinnamon
- Three quarters cup olive oil
- Two cups granulated sugar
- Three eggs
- Three quarters cup buttermilk
- Half tsp vanilla extract
- Two cups carrots, grated
- One can pineapple chunks
- One cup coconut flakes
- Twelve oz cream cheese
- Three quarters cup butter, softened
- Sixteen oz powdered sugar
- One cup pecans, chopped
- Ground nutmeg, to taste
- Cooking spray

Steps

- Mix in a bowl baking soda, flour, cinnamon, salt, olive oil & sugar. In another bowl beat with an electric mixer the eggs, vanilla & buttermilk until creamy. With the mixer working on medium speed slowly add the flour mixture until combined.
- Add to the bowl 8 oz pineapple chunks, the carrots & flaked coconut. Mix well. Spray a cookie sheet with the nonstick cooking spray & pour the cake batter into it.
- When ready to cook, set the grill temperature to 350°F, then keep the lid closed for 15 minutes.
- Transfer the cake directly on the grill grates & cook for 25-30 minutes or until a toothpick inserted in the center of the cake comes out clean.

- Remove from oven & set aside to cool while preparing the frosting.
- Prepare the frosting. in a mixer equipped with a paddle attachment, whip the cream cheese & butter until smooth. Gradually incorporate the powdered sugar till the mixture is soft & fluffy. Mix in the vanilla extract.
- Once the carrot cake has cooled, spread the cream cheese frosting on the surface. Sprinkle with sliced pecans & ground nutmeg. Slice as desired & serve.

9.6 Baked Apple Tart

Preparation time: 35 minutes

Cooking time: 30 minutes

Servings: 4

Ingredients

- Half cup all-purpose flour
- Three quarters cup butter
- Three apples
- Three tbsp granulated sugar
- Four tbsp dark sugar, divided
- One pinch ground cinnamon
- One tsp corn starch
- One pinch salt
- Two tbsp milk

Steps

- In a large mixing bowl, mix the flour & butter till it looks like cornmeal. Add 2 tbsp water & mix again.
- Roll the dough in plastic wrap & refrigerate for 30 minutes.
- Peel, core & dice the apples. Mix the apple dices with three tbsp brown sugar, butter, cornstarch, cinnamon & salt.
- When ready to cook, set the grill temperature to 325°F, then keep the lid closed for 15 minutes.
- Lightly flour a cutting board & roll the chilled dough into a ¼-inch thick round shape. In the middle, put the apple mixture. Fold the corners inward to close the tart.
- Now, drizzle the top of with some milk & sprinkle with the leftover dark sugar.

- Transfer the tart to a cookie sheet lined with parchment paper & place the cookie sheet onto the grill grates.
- Bake the tart for 25 - 30 minutes, until the dough is completely cooked.
- Remove the tart from the grill, let cool a bit & serve warm with whipped cream or ice cream.

9.7 Pumpkin Pie with Whisky Whipped Cream

Preparation time: 10 minutes

Cooking time: 50 minutes

Servings: 6

Ingredients

- One frozen pie crust
- Fifteen oz canned pumpkin
- Fourteen oz sweet condensed milk
- Half tsp pumpkin pie spices
- Half tsp vanilla extract
- One pinch salt
- Two eggs
- One cup heavy cream
- Two tbsp powdered sugar
- Two tsp bourbon whisky

Steps

- Thaw the pie crust. Combine the cream, pumpkin, pumpkin pie spices, vanilla & salt in a mixing bowl. Whip with an electric mixer. Add the eggs & whip again until completely mixed. Transfer the filling into the pie crust.
- Set the grill temperature to 425°F, then keep the lid closed for 15 minutes.
- Bake the pie for 15 minutes.
- Reduce the grill temperature to 350°F & bake for 35–40 more minutes, until a toothpick inserted in the center of the cake comes out clean.
- Using a hand mixer whip the cream till soft peaks form. Whip in the sugar, whiskey & vanilla extract until thoroughly mixed. Do not overmix.

- Remove the pie from the grill & let cool a bit. Serve the pie warm long with the whipped cream.

9.8 Honey Cornbread Cake

Preparation time: 10 minutes

Cooking time: 40 minutes

Servings: 6

Ingredients

- Two thirds cup olive oil
- Half cup buttermilk
- Four large eggs
- Five tbsp butter, melted
- Half cup mayonnaise
- Two tbsp honey
- Three cups all-purpose flour
- Two tbsp baking powder
- One tsp salt
- One cup cornmeal
- Half cup granulated sugar

Steps

- When ready to cook set the grill temperature to 350°F, then keep the lid closed for 15 minutes.
- Combine the buttermilk, olive oil, melted butter, eggs, mayonnaise & honey in a mixing bowl. Mix thoroughly & set aside.
- In another bowl combine the sugar, flour, baking powder, cornmeal & salt.
- Fold the wet & dry products together to blend, taking care not to overmix. Grease a 9x13-inches baking dish.
- Pour the mixture in the baking dish, transfer to the grill grates & bake for 35-40 minutes, until the cake top begins to brown & crack.
- Remove the baking dish from grill & let cool a bit. Serve warm with butter & honey.

9.9 Baked Rhubarb Cobbler

Preparation time: 15 minutes

Cooking time: 30 minutes

Servings: 6

Filling

- Half cup sugar
- Two tbsp quick tapioca
- Four cups fresh rhubarb, diced
- One pinch salt
- Three cups strawberries, diced
- One tbsp Grand Marnier

Crust

- One egg
- Four tbsp heavy cream
- A few drops almond extract
- A few drops vanilla extract
- One cup all-purpose flour
- Half tsp baking powder
- Half tsp cinnamon
- One pinch salt
- Four tbsp butter, chilled

- Generously grease a baking dish or casserole & set aside.
- Prepare the filling. Addo the tapioca sugar & salt to a large mixing bowl. Stir in the diced strawberries, diced rhubarb & orange liqueur. Mix with a rubber spatula & set aside.
- Prepare the crust. In another bowl whisk together the egg, salt, vanilla & almond extracts. In a third bowl combine the sugar, flour, cinnamon, baking powder & salt. Add the butter & work flour mixture until coarse

crumbs develop. Toss the flour with a fork & stir in milk & egg mixture until just mixed.

- Pour the fruit & any juices into the baking dish or ramekins previously prepared. Dollop batter on top in an even layer. Sprinkle additional sugar on top, if desired
- When ready to cook set the grill temperature to 350°F, then keep the lid closed for 15 minutes.
- Arrange the baking dish or ramekins directly on the grill grates & bake for 30-35 minutes, util the filling gets bubbling & the crust gets golden brown. Remove from the grill, let cool for a bit & serve.

9.10 Tarte Tatin

- Two cups all-purpose flour
- One tsp salt
- One cup plus four tbsp butter, divided
- Three quarters cup granulated sugar
- Ten apples, peeled & wedged

- When ready to cook set the grill temperature to 350°F, then keep the lid closed for 15 minutes.
- Prepare the crust. Add salt & flour in a food processor until combined. Add one cup of butter, a small amount at a time, pulsing to combine. When it looks like cornmeal, add 5 tbsp water & process until the dough comes together. Shape a round, roll it in plastic wrap & refrigerate.
- Add butter & sugar to a 10-inches baking dish, transfer to the grill grates & let caramelize.
- Remove the dish from the grill & cover the caramelized sugar with apple wedges in a fan shape.
- Cut a circle out of the pie crust wide enough to cover the dish. Cover the plate with the pastry dough & prick it with a fork. Allow for shrinkage when trimming the crust.

- Transfer the apple pie back on the grill & cook for 55 minutes, until the apples are fork tender. Remove from the grill, let rest for 3 minutes, place a plate over the pie & turn it over while the pan is still wet.
- Serve warm, with whipped cream or ice cream.

9.11 Oatmeal Chocolate Cookies

Preparation time: 10 minutes

Cooking time: 10 minutes

Servings: 8

Ingredients

- Three quarters cup brown sugar
- Half cup sugar
- One cup butter, softened
- One tsp vanilla extract
- One egg
- Two cups rolled oats
- Half cup all-purpose flour
- One tsp baking soda
- One tsp salt
- One cup chocolate chips

Steps

- When ready to cook set the grill temperature to 350°F, then keep the lid closed for 15 minutes.
- In a big mixing bowl mix the sugars & butter until smooth. Add the egg & vanilla extract & whisk until light & fluffy.
- Add the oats, all-purpose flour, baking soda, chocolate chips & salt. Mix well to combine
- Drop dough tablespoons onto a parchment-lined cookie sheet, spacing them about 2-inches apart.
- Transfer the sheet to the grill grates & cook till golden brown, about 10-12 minutes. Let cool slightly, then transfer to a wire rack & let cool completely before serving.

9.12 Baked Apple Pudding

Preparation time: 25 minutes

Cooking time: 1 hour

Servings: 6

Ingredients

- Half cup dried cranberries
- One tbsp candied ginger, chopped
- Four tbsp apple cider
- Six oz cream cheese
- Three tbsp brown sugar
- Two tbsp butter
- Half tsp vanilla extract
- Half tsp ground cinnamon
- One pinch ground nutmeg
- Four tbsp walnuts, chopped
- Six crispy apples
- Walnuts halves, for serving

Steps

- Pour the apple cider over the cranberries & ginger in a small bowl. Let the mixture to steep 30 minutes before draining. Reserve the apple cider.
- When ready to cook set the grill temperature to 350°F, then keep the lid closed for 15 minutes.
- Combine the brown sugar, cream cheese, vanilla extract, butter, cinnamon & nutmeg in a medium mixing, mixing until creamy. Add the chopped walnuts, cranberries & ginger, mixing again.
- Core the apples starting at the stem & working the way down, leaving the lower section intact. Fill the apples with the filling.
- Arrange the stuffed apples in a baking dish upright. Pour the reserved apple cider in the base of the dish.
- Cook the apples for 45-60 minutes, basting them with apple cider occasionally. Serve warm with walnut halves on top.